DRIVING UNDER THE INFLUENCE

DRIVING UNDER THE INFLUENCE

Finding Your Way on the Road of Life

SHUNDRAWN A. THOMAS

Cover photo provided courtesy of iStockPhoto.com/clintspencer(© Clint Spencer.)

Cover and Interior Design & Layout by Brian Taylor, Pneuma Books, LLC
For more info on Pneuma Books, visit www.pneumabooks.com

Publisher's Cataloging-in-Publication Data
(Prepared by The Donohue Group)

Thomas, Shundrawn A.
    Driving under the influence : finding your way on the road of life / Shundrawn A. Thomas.

    p. cm.
    LCCN 2010922358
    ISBN-13: 978-0-615-35031-8
    ISBN-10: 0-615-35031-3

    1. Christian life.   I. Title.

BV4501.3.S58 2010   248.4
               QBI10-600070

PRINTED IN THE UNITED STATES OF AMERICA
on acid∞free paper
17 16 15 14 13 12 11 10   01 02 03 04 05 06 07 08

This book is dedicated to the Saul of Tarsus
who demonstrated that on the road of life,
God does allow u-turns.

●

This book is likewise dedicated to my fellow drivers
currently enroute to your God-ordained destination.
Let His Spirit be your guide and like the born-again Saul,
you will successfully complete your course.

Contents

Preface

The question seems simple enough. Why did I write this book? The answer, as it turns out, is not so simple. While this may come as a surprise, it is not necessarily a question one considers at the start of a project. Sometimes, as in this case, you simply go as the Spirit moves you. That's how it happens for me anyway. For me, writing is a vocation as opposed to an occupation. It started as a child with an interest in writing short stories and poetry. Though I did not pursue writing as a profession, I often found excuses to exercise my latent gift.

Now there is the matter of this particular book. It is the third of what I hope will be many. I am, as the subtitle aptly states, finding my way on the road of life. As I've made my way on this personal journey, I've often pondered philosophical questions about life. Why am I here? Where am I headed? Who will help me find my way? Maybe you've pondered these questions as well.

It could be said that the meaning of life depends on your vantage point. My reason for writing this book is simply to share my perspective. Sharing by definition is a generous act, but my aim is not entirely selfless. My first objective in considering this weighty matter is to bring clarity to my own journey. It is through the prism of my own life experience, however imperfect, that I hope to help others find their own way.

I cannot attest that I've produced a literary masterpiece or a best-seller. Those sorts of things are for others to surmise. Recognition never was nor ever will be my motivation. My ultimate objective for writing this book is to share an essential truth as best I know it. God is real, and He desires to live inside of us. I know because He is alive in me. When we allow God's Spirit to come alive in us, He not only guides us but inspires us.

To many, the thought of being guided by God's Spirit is a bit unnerving. It takes faith to live in that manner. But that of course is the rub. Faith is a term often used but seldom put into practice. People who live by faith occasionally do seemingly odd things, like writing books for passion as opposed to purse strings.

Now I've answered the question as to why I wrote this book. Why you've peeked between the covers is another matter altogether. I trust that in some way God's Spirit is speaking to you. I gave in and wrote the book. You might as well give in and read it. May God guide and keep you as you find your way on the road of life.

Your fellow traveler,
Shundrawn A. Thomas

Introduction – The Road Ahead

"How can we understand the road we travel?
It is the Lord who directs our steps."
Proverbs 20:24, NLT

Early one Saturday morning I left my home, headed to an appointment in the city. Traffic on the freeway normally moved swiftly at that hour, and I was surprised when traffic slowed to a halt. I hadn't anticipated the delay and immediately began to bemoan the prospect of being late for my appointment. After observing a number of drivers exiting the freeway, I followed their example in search of an alternate route. I found myself in a deliberate procession of vehicles on a single lane boulevard. As I turned onto a major street, I assumed my fortunes had changed. I did a mental check to recalculate the route to my destination and was on my way.

Just as it seemed that my trip was back on course, I encountered my second detour. A freight train had stalled, blocking a key thoroughfare that I'd planned to take. After several minutes and no activity from the train, I decided to revise my route yet again. This latest revision required me to retrace my path, taking a two-mile detour. Despite the delays, I figured I could get to my appointment about ten minutes behind schedule. I simply needed to hop on a different freeway that would allow me to exit near my destination. As I approached the on ramp, you can likely guess what happened next. I encountered my third detour of the morning. Construction had begun the previous day and several local ramps were closed.

After a parade of red lights I arrived at my destination, albeit twenty minutes late for my appointment. While patience is not my strongest suit, I was more amused than agitated. I considered how I regularly get behind the wheel without considering the possibility of delays. I also considered how my choice to blindly follow others resulted in numerous detours and even a dead end. I thought about how much easier my trip would have been had I checked the traffic report. Better still, I considered how much easier my trip would have been if I had a guide to provide me with insight into the road and traffic conditions ahead. Once I returned home and reflected on my morning, I knew exactly how I'd begin this manuscript.

Road Test

King Solomon penned a proverb that asks a simple yet profound question: How *do* we find our way on the road of life? Solomon's question is rhetorical and is followed by his declaration that God determines our way. Solomon's proverb brings to light one of the most essential questions in the human experience. Is my life headed in the right direction? I've spent many hours pondering this question. I expect you have too. Maybe you're presently grappling with the same question. Maybe that's why you picked up this book.

In my endeavor to chart a course for my life, I've drawn some basic conclusions. Much like our fingerprints, the Creator has orchestrated human experiences such that no two are alike. For that reason, life is not an equation with a finite solution or a riddle with an exact answer. It is instead a journey meant to be completed. While my life involves others by design and necessity, the path I inevitably must travel is unique to me. The same is true for you.

Inasmuch as God is the choreographer of the human experience, His presence is the only thing that gives life true meaning. This simple truth is the most important conclusion of all. While the world is littered with temporal pleasures, life is a hollow experience apart from God. God never intended to be a distant observer of our lives but rather an active participant. This is why He offers us the gift of His indwelling Spirit.

Blind Ambition

> *"'What shall I do, Lord?' I asked. 'Get up,' the Lord said, 'and go into Damascus. There you will be told all that you have been assigned to do.'"*
> *Acts 22:10, NIV*

The Apostle Paul is considered by many to be the greatest evangelist of all time. His dramatic conversion and tireless dedication to the cause of Christ demonstrate the profound impact that an individual can have when led by God's Spirit. Paul (known as Saul among Jews) was born in Tarsus, which is located in the Southwest region of modern day Turkey. His parents were devout Jews as well as Pharisees. The Pharisees were a religious sect distinguished for their strict interpretation of the Mosaic Law. Paul's family was well off and likely purchased their Roman citizenship. The privileges conferred from Roman citizenship would prove essential for the path that Paul's life would inevitably take.

Paul likely spent a good portion of his adolescent years in the synagogue mastering Jewish history, literature, poetry and psalms. It was under the careful tutelage of the renowned teacher Gamaliel that Paul gained his deep understanding of the Holy Scriptures. He also learned to debate in the question-and-answer style that was practiced by Pharisees and scribes (lawyers) as well as philosophers in the ancient world. By all accounts Paul was naturally curious and had a powerful intellect. These traits served the young Pharisee well as he tested his ability to expound, defend and prosecute the law.

Paul's zeal and intellect outpaced many of his contemporaries. Though Paul's early ambitions are not explicitly divulged in scripture, it is reasonable to believe the young Pharisee had his heart set on the Sanhedrin. The Sanhedrin was a seventy-one member body comprised of priests, rabbis and lawyers who were deemed experts in the Law of Moses. Although there were local magistrates, or governors, set in place by the Romans, religious matters as well as certain civil matters were adjudicated by the Sanhedrin. Whatever his true ambition, it motivated Paul's tireless prosecution of the followers of Jesus of Nazareth.

The movement known as "the Way" was spreading rapidly in Jerusalem and its surrounding regions. The political leaders thought that the death of Jesus of Nazareth would put an end to what they considered a radical sect. However, with followers of Christ seemingly emboldened by His resurrection, certain religious leaders conspired to bring about a systematic suppression of the movement. The ambitious young Pharisee from Tarsus would serve as their chief agent. Many followers of Christ in Jerusalem were either driven into hiding or forced to move to the neighboring regions of Samaria, Syria and Phoenicia. Damascus, possibly the world's oldest city, attracted followers of "the way" and their assemblies quickly swelled. Paul set out for Damascus in order to suppress the spread of the gospel in this major commercial center.

A New Direction

On his journey to Damascus, Paul was accompanied by a small caravan that included temple guards. The company was traveling about noon when a light Paul describes as more brilliant than the sun flashed around them. The light accompanied a presence that was both inexplicable and terrifying, causing the group of travelers to fall to the ground. From this point forward only Paul is acutely aware of the presence as well as the authoritative voice he would hear next.

'Saul, Saul, why do you persecute me?'

Paul mustered all of his strength and meekly replied, 'Who are you, Lord?'

'I am Jesus of Nazareth, whom you are persecuting,' the Lord replied.

Afraid and bewildered, Paul asked, 'What shall I do, Lord?'

'Get up and go into Damascus.' Jesus replied. 'There you will be told all that you have been assigned to do.' With those instructions, Jesus departed as suddenly as He'd appeared.

As Paul struggled to his feet, he realized that he'd lost his sight. His sudden loss of physical sight amplified the thoughts that raced in his head. Paul had fiercely opposed the followers of what he deemed a counterfeit religion only to find that Jesus of Nazareth was indeed the long awaited Messiah. This stark revelation of the truth must have made the remainder of the trip to Damascus seem like an eternity. How did I lose my way? Why was I so blind to the truth? What will I do now? How will I find my way? These are the types of questions that Paul likely asked himself on that forlorn road to Damascus.

Once he arrived in Damascus, Paul spent three days fasting and praying. While Paul immersed himself in prayer, Jesus worked on his behalf. Ananias was a respected member of the Jewish community and a follower of "the way". Jesus appeared to Ananias in a vision and instructed him to minister to Paul. Ananias affirmed Paul's assignment to preach to the Gentile nations. When Ananias laid hands on Paul, he immediately recovered his sight. Paul also received the gift of the Holy Spirit. Paul now had the driving force that he needed to venture down the new road that lay ahead of him.

Let the Spirit Move You

Have you ventured down Damascus road? In other words, have you had a life-changing experience that's caused you to realize that your life is headed in the wrong direction? Maybe it's more subtle in your case. You've simply come to a proverbial fork in the road and you're torn between two or more paths. Maybe you've run into an unexpected road block. Should you turn back or choose an alternate route to your destination? Maybe unresolved doubts or fears have impeded your progress. If you can identify with any of the situations I've just described, I've got some good news to share.

God desires to live on the inside of you. All you have to do is open your heart. Submission to His will is the ultimate act of humility. It also gives Him the right to get involved in your daily affairs. Life truly is an adventure and only God knows the twists and turns that await you. That makes Him your perfect Guide. The Bible describes the Holy Spirit as our comforter or helper and He designed life's journey with the expectation of assisting us along the way.

Life without God is epitomized by activity without real progress... transition without true change... and good without actual gain. After his conversion Paul remarked that everything else was worthless when compared to the gain of knowing Christ Jesus (Phil. 3:8). Life without God's Spirit is not living life to the fullest because His presence ultimately gives life's journey meaning. We often relegate God's influence to religious gatherings or practices. This limited understanding leaves us unfulfilled in our daily lives. Wouldn't it be better to experience life the way God intended it? Then we must allow God's presence to be prevalent in our daily lives.

The road of life is full of unexpected twists and turns. Along the way we encounter delays, detours, and the occasional dead end. Interestingly enough, the experiences gained and the lessons learned are at times the very things that make life worth living. The Holy Spirit serves as our internal guide, enabling us to maximize our individual experience and confidently find our way on the road of life. This personal revelation caused me to accept the vital necessity of what I refer to as *Driving Under the Influence*.

I've come to understand that God's Spirit is the necessary ingredient for a truly satisfying life. The Spirit gives us access to the heart of God, enabling us to see the world from His perspective. When we allow God's Spirit to live on the inside, His character and His ways guide our decisions. That is the essence of *Driving Under the Influence*. It's about recognizing the unique assignments and abilities that God has given you. More importantly, it's about allowing the Holy Spirit to rule your heart and govern your life. I pray that God's Spirit invades your heart as never before as you find your way along the road of life.

●

Part

1

Prepare for Your Journey

"Do you not know that those who run in a race all run,
but only one receives the prize? Run in such a way that you may win."
1 Corinthians 9:24, NASB

Though chiefly associated with Christian doctrine, the preserved letters of the Apostle Paul are some of the greatest literary works ever composed. As a result of his dramatic conversion, Paul's perspective on life was totally transformed. Paul's letters inspire his readers to undergo a similar transformation with regard to their perspective of life. Paul's views can be summarized in a statement that he made before an esteemed council of philosophers in Athens, Greece. "In God we live and move and exist," Paul remarked to his listeners (Acts 17:28). This statement epitomized Paul's attitude toward his own life and the attitude he attempted to cultivate in others.

In his first letter to the Corinthians, Paul provides great insight into life's journey. Corinth was the site of the Isthmian Games, a great athletic festival. (Think of it as a cousin to our modern-day Olympic Games.) Corinth was a popular venue because it was one of the oldest, largest and wealthiest cities of ancient Greece. First established by the Greeks in 581 B.C, the Isthmian Games drew spectators and contestants from all over the world. Following a hiatus, the Isthmian games were reestablished by Julius Caesar following the Roman conquest of the Greeks. Prospective contestants were required to complete at least ten months of training prior to the games. Those who failed to complete the training were barred from the competition.

The illustration would have been especially poignant to his readers who were likely spectators of the athletic festival. Physical fitness and athletic prowess were highly prized in Greek and Roman culture. As such, Paul's readers took the games very seriously. While contestants generally competed in numerous events, the highlight of the games was an endurance race. It was this race in particular that Paul alludes to in his letter to the Corinthians. The victor's prize was a crown of pine or wild celery that symbolized athletic excellence.

Paul noted that while a number of competitors qualified for the race, only one ultimately received the victor's wreath. The operative word is *qualified*. Only the fittest contestants were deemed qualified to participate in the competition. This underscores the importance of proper training and preparation. Whether in a team sport or an individual contest, success comes as a result of the painstaking work done prior to competition. This is especially true in an endurance race, such as a marathon. Only those who train faithfully have the stamina to endure to the end.

Paul encourages us to live our lives with the same type of focus and determination that contestants exhibit in an endurance race. The implication being that we will likewise receive a reward if we persevere to the end. Unfortunately, many of us drift through life as spectators, failing to prepare for the road ahead. In some cases, we lack the desire to seek God's will; and in others, we lack the commitment to make the sacrifice that God requires. The perplexing fact is that most of us expend significant energy on work and other activities. However, without God's direction, we are left without a clear path or destination.

In order to successfully navigate the road of life we must begin with proper preparation. This involves seeking God's will, determining our destination, broadening our perspective, and charting our course. Similar to training for an endurance race, these activities articulate the necessary regimen that qualifies us for life's journey. And while preparation alone does not guarantee success, it sets us on the path toward the victor's prize.

Throughout this book I will use an analogy of a road trip in an automobile to illuminate spiritual truths regarding life's journey. I will also use this analogy to share perspective and experiences from my individual course. My ultimate objective is to reinforce the supposition that the presence and leading of God's Spirit is what gives life true meaning. In the first section of the book we will focus on the training regimen alluded to earlier. It is my belief that careful attention to these foundational steps will position you to successfully complete the course that God has set before you. Let's begin our journey of *Driving Under the Influence*.

●

①

Are You a Passenger or a Driver?

"If we are living now by the Holy Spirit,
let us follow the Holy Spirit's leading in every part of our lives."
Galatians 5:25, NLT

In 1995, the German automobile manufacturer Volkswagen launched one of the most successful advertising campaigns of all time. The company boldly proclaimed that "on the road of life there are passengers and there are drivers." The implication being that some people are content to allow things to simply happen while other people take control of their lives. Strategically targeted to baby boomer children (Generation X), the campaign was both provocative and profound, reaching a vital audience that advertisers had struggled to connect with.

The advertising campaign persisted for over a decade, with Volkswagen only recently shifting their theme. The longevity and effectiveness of the ad campaign eclipsed the appeal of the manufacturer's automobiles. While the advertising agency has been lauded for the ingenious campaign, I'd argue that there was another subtle factor that greatly contributed to the success. The campaign appealed to a powerful and at times dormant desire in each of us. The desire to master our destiny, or to become drivers as Volkswagen aptly put it, is the essence of the human spirit. It is a defining characteristic that makes us like God, our Father.

While the mastery of one's destiny is desirable and attainable, it paradoxically cannot be accomplished through our limited human abilities. The inner working of God's Spirit empowers us to take control of our lives. The Apostle Paul understood this truth through personal experience as opposed to mental ascent. People often attempt to find their way in life apart from God — equating free choice with free reign. Paul cautions his readers of the arrogance and danger of such thinking. In what is believed to be Paul's first general epistle, Paul makes an impassioned defense of faith in Jesus Christ. Paul concludes that only the power of His Spirit can preserve us on the road of life.

Faith in Jesus Christ and the power of His Spirit were the central themes of Paul's message to the Galatians. Paul became aware that individuals were distorting his message through alternative teaching. Some placed emphasis on good deeds while others placed emphasis on philosophy. Paul feared that the Galatians would abandon their early faith, relying instead on human effort and intellect. The influences that the Galatians considered are analogous to influences we encounter today. Modern philosophy and self-help rhetoric espouse the way to self-discovery and fulfillment in life. Though presumably well-meaning, these surrogates can shift our focus away from God, our true guide. Paul encourages us to place our trust in God and follow His Spirit's leading in every area of our lives. Only then can we truly master our destiny.

Early Adoption

"What I am saying is that as long as the heir is a child, he is no different from a slave, although he owns the whole estate. He is subject to guardians and trustees until the time set by his father. So also, when we were children, we were in slavery under the basic principles of the world." Galatians 4:1-3, NIV

In order to appreciate Paul's letter to the Galatians, it is helpful to understand the context of his communication. It is believed that Paul evangelized the region of Galatia in his early travels or during what is known as his first missionary journey. The region, part of modern-day Turkey, was not far from Paul's birthplace of Tarsus. Paul became ill during his visit to the region and subsequently stayed much longer than he intended. Despite his failing health and weak condition, he continued to share his message, convincing many people to become followers of Christ. Paul visited the Galatians on later trips and regularly checked on their welfare. As such, Paul was very disheartened to hear that his beloved Galatians appeared to stray from their course.

Though passionate in his response, Paul's reproof was born out of love, not anger. To effectively make his case, Paul employed the analogy of a young heir to an estate. From the moment of birth, the child is part owner of the family's estate. Paul notes that during the time leading up to maturity, the child's status differs little from a slave's. Although the child is the heir of the estate, he or she can't exercise any rights with respect to the property until the time determined by the parent. The child's life is governed by guardians and tutors who are responsible for the child until the point of maturity. It is important to note that the term *child* that is used by Paul means immature one and was generally used to describe a minor or young adult.

The term *adoption*, to which Paul refers, differs from the common definition employed in most modern cultures. The modern definition generally involves voluntarily taking a child as one's own. Adoption, in the context of Paul's letter, referred to the public attestation of adulthood. A father publicly proclaimed that his child had reached the level of maturity. There were both social and legal implications to this important distinction. At maturity or adoption, a child received legal authority over his or her inheritance. The term *son* is gender neutral in the Greek language and at times was used interchangeably with the term *child*. However, a strict definition of *son* referenced an heir who received the distinction of adoption. As such, the use of the term *son* in the Bible often carries a subtle but important distinction.

The legal distinction of maturity was not age-based, as is common in modern law. It was instead a right exclusively conferred by the father or grantor of the estate. The father determined whether the child was mature enough to rightly manage his or her inheritance. At such time as determined by the father, the child received privileges and responsibilities that were formerly the sole domain of the father. This is why only the father retained the authority to confer the distinction.

Paul teaches us that prior to maturing in the area of faith, we are governed by the basic principles of the world. In other words, external circumstances and influences dictate our course in life – thereby relegating us to the role of passenger. Our daily lives are similar to the minor who exercises little control over his or her destiny until a seminal event occurs. This event is known as spiritual adoption.

Have you ever found yourself in a situation that caused you to feel helpless or confused? A better question might be, how often do you find yourself in such situations? If you are a passionate person like me, you may often find yourself in challenging circumstances. Paul informs us that the Holy Spirit not only gives us the power to manage difficult circumstances but also gives us insight to help us make sound decisions along the way.

While it is true that the Holy Spirit empowers us to manage life's circumstances, we must also appreciate the other essential function that God's Spirit plays in our lives. The influence of the Holy Spirit causes us to mature with respect to our faith in God. The Holy Spirit also helps us to understand God's Word and gives us insight into our own character. This is a point that we will discuss extensively in later chapters. It is at maturity that the power of God freely operates through our lives. The more we learn about God's Word, the more we trust Him. The more we trust God, the more success we have navigating the road of life.

Driver's Education

One of the highlights of my sophomore year in high school was enrolling in driver's education class. This rite of passage offered to teenage students in the United States public school system includes classroom training and numerous hours behind the wheel of a simulator. It's funny in retrospect, but I really looked forward to getting behind the wheel of those worn-out simulators at the driver's education facility. Once the instructor turned down the lights and started the video rolling, I'd easily forget I was in a stationary machine.

After five weeks of classroom testing and simulation driving, it was off to the road course. In my case, the road course was a school parking lot with a maze of orange cones. The instructor would climb in next to the student driver. There was an emergency brake conveniently installed on the passenger side in the event an inexperienced student veered outside of the carefully arranged cones. As an additional precaution, the accelerators were rigged so that the vehicle would not exceed twenty miles per hour. We spent the next five weeks honing our skills on the course and practicing maneuvers such as parallel parking. The ten-week program culminated with both a written test and a road test.

Although I passed with flying colors, the reward was somewhat anticlimatic. I hadn't reached my sixteenth birthday, the legal age to drive in my locality. So like the majority of graduates in my class, I received a learner's permit. A learner's permit confers certain limited privileges but it should in no way be confused with a driver's license. In short, the holder of a learner's permit is only allowed to get behind the wheel of a car if accompanied by a licensed adult driver. Moreover, the licensed adult driver is responsible for supervising the learner and ultimately responsible for his or her actions behind the wheel.

Although I enjoyed limited rights, including the occasional spin around the block, I was not legally considered a driver. Anytime I got behind the wheel of a car, I was under the careful supervision of an adult driver (usually my father). I was not ultimately responsible for my actions behind the wheel of the car. Add to this the fact that I neither owned a vehicle nor paid auto insurance, and it was clear that I was a passenger and not a driver.

I learned quickly that operating a motor vehicle doesn't necessarily qualify me as a driver. There are certain requirements that must be met, such as obtaining a license. There are certain responsibilities that must be managed, such as the note and the insurance premium. Experience must be gained under the careful supervision of proven drivers. Finally, the driver must have a purpose and a destination in mind or he or she is no different from a passenger.

Back Down Memory Lane

I'll never forget turning sixteen. The first thing on my mind was obtaining my driver's license. I hounded my father every day until he took me to the Department of Motor Vehicles. After taking the official road test, I finally received my driver's license. My birthday was late in the year so many of my close friends had already obtained their driver's license. I was overjoyed to finally be part of the club. I'd soon learn that obtaining a license doesn't necessarily make you an effective driver.

Shortly after obtaining my license, my father helped me purchase my first automobile, a used 1983 Oldsmobile Omega. Although used family cars and teenage tastes don't generally mix, I was ecstatic to have a car of my own. As I pulled off the dealership lot, I felt an enormous sense of pride. But as I made a left turn across traffic, I misjudged the oncoming traffic and it happened.

I crashed into the side of an oncoming car. I was literally a stone's throw from the dealership, which added insult to my vehicle's injury. Fortunately, the damage to both vehicles was limited, but the lesson I learned was significant. Even though I'd obtained a license and owned an automobile, I wasn't a proficient driver. Proficiency would only be achieved through practice, experience, and careful attention to the rules of the road. We will discuss this topic in greater detail later in the text.

It took me six weeks to save up the money to pay for the damage I caused. The experience taught me an early lesson about the responsibility that comes with operating an automobile. My life experience has been similar. As a young adult I ventured out into the world believing that I had a full-proof plan and a license to drive. While parts of my adult life thus far have been fruitful and rewarding, I've had my fair share of mishaps and near misses. I've come to realize the vital importance of having a clear destination and proper guidance along the way. I now realize more than ever that I need the strength that comes from a power greater than my own.

Drivers Wanted

We began the chapter by citing the venerable Volkswagen advertising campaign that declared that "on the road of life there are passengers and drivers."

Those familiar with the campaign are also aware of the tagline that followed this declaration. The tagline simply read "Drivers Wanted." This simple yet powerful phrase defined the campaign. In many respects, the phrase was an open invitation to anyone who wants to be a driver. The implication being that Volkswagen, through its product offering, could enable the consumer to achieve this distinction. The ad invited the individual to be a part of a club that by inference was distinguished or unique. After all, everyone wouldn't choose to purchase a Volkswagen. In the same respect, everyone who goes through life won't choose to be a driver.

You may have never thought of it this way, but God advertises in a similar fashion. God extends an open invitation and as you might have guessed, His Word effectively declares that He is seeking drivers. Jesus personalized this by stating that anyone who desires can simply follow His lead (Mark 8:34). God does not simply advertise or invite us, but He actively seeks to empower us. The Word of God declares that God is constantly searching for those whose hearts are committed to Him in order to strengthen them (2 Chron. 16:9). The benefit is clear. God offers us the ability to take control of our destiny through the inner working of His Spirit.

The benefits that accrue from our relationship with God do not come without responsibility. In the same way that we must obtain a license to drive, we must mature in spiritual matters. Specifically, we must exhibit the character traits of Jesus Christ: love, joy, peace, patience, kindness, goodness, faithfulness, gentleness and self-control. This maturation allows us to effectively make our way on the road of life. Spiritual growth also gives God greater occasion to intervene in our lives. Jesus alluded to this in a discussion with His followers. He told them that they would perform even greater works than He'd performed because He was going to be with the Father. He promised that He would send His Spirit, which would make the great works He foreshadowed possible.

I remember when I personally responded to God's invitation. I wasn't in dire straits... at least not by common standards. I enjoyed a successful career and a very comfortable lifestyle. My longing, however, was not for success. It was instead an intense longing for significance. The education, career, finances, and even friendships didn't fill the void I felt deep down. More importantly, I wasn't in control. I don't say this to imply that my lifestyle was reckless. In fact, it was quite the contrary. My life was very regimented and controlled. As Paul aptly put it, I was a slave to the basic principles of this world. And that is why God's invitation was so appealing.

As I began to open up my heart to God, I received the message of the gospel in a whole new way. I knew that God had the power to deliver me from the bondage of sin. I had to learn that God had a purpose for my life. I only needed to accept His direction and He would lead me down a path of significance. It's incredible to know that the God of the universe is personally concerned about me. I'm one of the many drivers that He faithfully guides. His indwelling Spirit has transformed my life into a wonderful adventure that He orchestrates.

Maybe your experience is similar to mine. Maybe you are similarly looking for a transition from temporal success to lasting significance. Maybe God's invitation has touched your heart. Drivers wanted! Yes, He is speaking to you! In fact, He is calling out to you in the same way He calls each one of us. He invites us each on a wonderful journey that only begins when we truly invite Him into our hearts.

●

Chapter

2

Where Are You Headed?

"But if our gospel be hid, it is hid to them that are lost: in whom
the god of this world hath blinded the minds of them which believe not,
lest the light of the glorious gospel of Christ,
who is the image of God, should shine unto them."
2 Corinthians 4:3-4, KJV

In early 2009, the Broadway musical *Wicked* completed an open-ended run, which made it the top-grossing and longest-running musical in Chicago history. The plot of the musical is based on characters from the timeless children's novel *The Wonderful Wizard of Oz*. The fanfare around the musical brought back fond childhood memories of the 1939 film directed by Victor Fleming. During my adolescent years, the television screening of *The Wizard of Oz* was an annual family tradition. We'd huddle around the floor model television and somehow I never grew tired of watching the film.

The film's plot is simple. The protagonist, Dorothy Gale, is knocked unconscious during a tornado. In her dream, Dorothy and her dog, Toto, are transported to the magical Land of Oz. This turn of events is quite unsettling for Dorothy as she finds herself in a completely foreign place. Dorothy is completely and utterly lost. While it is true that Dorothy is unsure of her location, her real problem is that she doesn't know where she is headed.

The pivotal point of the story occurs when Glinda, the Good Witch of the North, directs Dorothy to go to Emerald City to meet the Wizard of Oz. The way to the Emerald City is, of course, paved by a yellow brick road. Glinda provides Dorothy with a sense of direction and purpose for her journey. With a destination in mind and purpose in her heart, Dorothy is no longer lost. Moreover, she meets others whom she is able to help and encourage during her journey.

When you woke up this morning, you certainly knew where you were. I'll bet you still do. But do you know where you are headed? What are your life goals? What is your ultimate destination and do you have a plan to get there? To be lost simply means to be unable to find one's way. It also means that you are beyond reach or influence. Despite the fact that there are nearly 6.8 billion people (and counting) on the planet, we each have a God-ordained journey to complete. Life's journey doesn't have a road map per se. The landscape is constantly changing. And while people and circumstances constantly change, your destination must be sure. The Holy Spirit gives us insight into life that can only be derived from God's perspective.

In Paul's second letter to the Corinthians he speaks of being separated from God's Spirit and blind to the truth of the Gospel. When we are unfamiliar with God's Word, we find ourselves lost or beyond His influence. The truth and instruction found in His Word is the key to His Spirit coming alive in us. When His Spirit is alive in us, our direction is clear because the essential truths of God's Word are revealed. That's why God's Word is vital to navigating the road of life. It doesn't explicitly tell you which way to go. It does, however, establish truths and principles that enable you to choose the right direction.

Heaven Sent

"While they were worshiping the Lord and fasting, the Holy Spirit said,
'Set apart for me Barnabas and Saul for the work to which I have called them.'

So after they had fasted and prayed, they placed their hands on them and sent them off." Acts 13:2-3, NIV

After his sojourn in Arabia, Paul returned to Damascus for an extended stay. A vibrant center of commerce, Damascus was a perfect training ground for his evangelistic ministry. Paul decided to travel to Jerusalem to meet with the leaders of the church. Paul was searching for clarity regarding his assignment and hoped that his return to Jerusalem would provide him with insight. Shortly after arriving in Jerusalem, Paul became acquainted with Barnabas who would later become a partner in ministry. Barnabas made it possible for Paul to join with the assembly in Jerusalem in spite of their apprehension over his former life. Paul's stay, however, was short-lived because he received a vision of Christ directing him to leave straight away. Paul is believed to have spent the next four to five years of his life in his birthplace of Tarsus.

Barnabas was dispatched from Jerusalem to oversee an assembly at Antioch, which was not far from Tarsus. Barnabas recruited Paul, believing that he would be a strong asset to the growing fellowship that was composed of many Gentiles. The Holy Spirit further developed Paul, using service as a tool to impart valuable lessons. This service was necessary to perfect the character traits befitting a godly leader. During a time of fasting and worship, the Holy Spirit spoke to the believers at Antioch, instructing them to send forth Paul and Barnabas for the assignment they'd been given. Though Paul had spent just over a year at Antioch, a decade had passed since his conversion. Paul was now ready to embark on his mission.

Final Destination

Paul's first missionary trip spanned about three years and 1,400 miles. During their travels through Galatia and Asia Minor (modern-day Syria and Turkey), Paul and Barnabas were led to ten different cities. Despite hardship, affliction, and opposition, they tirelessly pursued their calling to preach the gospel to the nations. Along the way, many souls were introduced to Christ and numerous local assemblies were established. Paul would repeat this pattern on future missionary trips, venturing into new places and recruiting co-workers to join his ministry team.

Paul's simple message was salvation through faith in Jesus Christ and the hope of eternity in His kingdom. Likewise, Paul's destination was the kingdom of God and eternity with Christ. Through the revelation of the Holy Spirit, Paul came to understand his God-given assignment. Paul's missions involved many stops along the way. However, his destination, as opposed to his temporal circumstances, defined his journey. Jesus changed Paul's life by changing his destination. Once God's destiny for his life was revealed, he was free from the sin and distractions that had previously blinded him. With clear vision he could find the right path and stay the course no matter what obstacles came his way.

Every journey begins and ends with a destination. The destination is what gives the journey meaning. Reaching it becomes the measure of true success. Many people wander through life without a clear destination or purpose. This is not to say that they don't have goals. However, goals are a far cry from destiny. Goals may produce ambition, but destiny produces passion. Paul pursued his course with such passion because for the first time in his life his destination was clear. Where are you headed? What destination has God ordained for you? Are you prepared to do what it takes to successfully arrive at your appointed destination?

In order to successfully travel down the road of life, we must know where we are going--our destination must be clear. This is not a matter of convenience, and we do not get to abstain from making a choice. Ultimately, we all will make the transition to eternity. The decisions we make during this present life will determine our final destination. Destiny, or God's preferred end for mankind, is the most important revelation to a traveler on the road of life. We are God's most prized creation and everything that God creates is eternal. Physics teaches us that matter is neither created nor destroyed, it simply changes state. Matter is the basic building material of the physical world. This basic material and all other complex materials were created by God to last for eternity. In like manner, we too are created for eternity. In turn, when we encounter physical death we simply change states. So the question is posed to you again. Where are you headed? Stated another way, where will you spend eternity?

Recall that life's journey is predicated on a clear destination. Your destination is critically important because it governs your attitude as well as your activities. Fulfillment comes from progress toward (and ultimately your arrival at) your appointed destination. Conversely, life is unfulfilling in the absence of a clear destination. The proper destination influences your daily choices because it draws your internal compass or heart in the right direction. It is commonly said that if you don't know where you are going, any route will take you there. However, the road to eternity is only successfully navigated under the careful leading of God's Spirit.

Know Your Assignment

I've heard a number enlightening viewpoints on the subject of destiny that have aided me in my personal journey. I've also heard many viewpoints that seem at odds with practical experience and inconsistent with the fundamental truths outlined in the Word of God. While I do not profess to fully comprehend the mysteries of life, the Holy Spirit has enriched my perspective of my own destiny. I believe that God gives me assignments in life. My ministry or service is the faithful fulfillment of my God-given assignments. These assignments are devised foremost to develop my faith and strengthen my relationship with God. They are also meant to enable me to ascertain and develop my God-given gifts. These skills or abilities when employed under the leading of the Spirit enable me to serve humanity in a way that brings glory to God. Inasmuch as God extends us all the same grace, I believe He works similarly in your life.

When we think of ministry in the context of our journey on the road of life, it is not as simple as completing a task. As Paul discovered, the road of life is in effect a series of intermediate destinations or stopovers that lead to one's ultimate destiny. As we alluded earlier, the road of life is dynamic. Our next stopover depends on a number of things. Sometimes it depends on the decision that we made at the last fork in the road. At other times it is a function of the level of maturity we exhibit as we follow God's instructions. Our route may depend on a passenger that we are destined to encounter down the road. Whatever the case, it is God's will that must ultimately prevail if we are to reach our final destination.

The dynamic nature of our assignments requires us to depend on God's wisdom and guidance. Wisdom is the ability to make the right choices (the operative word being *right*). True wisdom is imparted through God's Word, which establishes what is right. God's indwelling Spirit enables us to correctly interpret God's instructions and to discern His intent during difficult times. This is why I firmly believe that assignments are revealed by God, but the route we travel must be discovered. God gives us assignments to help us down the path to self-discovery. Seeking His will helps us to discover our purpose. Pursuing our purpose gives meaning to life's journey. We must have faith in our assignments and more importantly our assignor.

Take Your Place

As Paul traveled from place to place carrying out his assignment, he constantly spoke of the kingdom of God. This should make perfect sense because Paul was merely telling others about his destination. Paul was so convinced that God's kingdom was mankind's ultimate destiny he wanted to share this good news or gospel with any and everyone. Although many people think of the gospel concerning God's kingdom in a religious context, it is a universal message. Its essence is simply about God's destiny for all of mankind.

If we come to understand that the gospel is about destiny and not about religion, it gives us an entirely different perspective on our journey in life. God imparts principles and laws for the natural world through His Word. When we apply His principles and obey His laws, we effectively navigate the road of life. This is why sin or disobedience is a critical issue in our lives. Sin separates us from God, our source of direction and provision on the road of life. The simple truth is that sin keeps us from our destiny, while obedience leads us to our destiny. We must rightly apply God's Word to our unique circumstances.

Have you made God's kingdom your destination on the road of life? This is not a question of religious practices or church affiliation. It is, however, a question of allegiance to the Spirit of God. As you follow God's Spirit on the road of life, you are assured of an experience that is unique to you. And while all believers travel in the same direction, our paths and experiences differ greatly. As I have traveled on my personal journey, I've learned to appreciate the assignments God has revealed for me – even though I didn't desire or comprehend them at times. With maturity I've learned to simply ask what He would have me learn or do. Jesus promised to prepare a place for us in His eternal kingdom and this promise is sure. If we have faith in Him and obey His Word, His Spirit will lead us to the place He has prepared.

•

Can You
See the
Destination?

"The man without the Spirit does not accept the things that come from the Spirit of God, for they are foolishness to him, and he cannot understand them, because they are spiritually discerned." 1 Corinthians 2:14, NIV

The 1999 Film *The Sixth Sense* tells the story of Cole Sear, a troubled boy, who has what he believes is a dark secret. His mother, a single parent, is emotionally distraught trying to deal with Cole's unconventional behavior. Dr. Malcolm Crowe, a child psychologist, tries to help Cole deal with his problem. The film centers on their interactions and budding relationship. As Dr. Crowe establishes rapport with Cole, he wins his trust. The pivotal scene of the movie is when Cole reveals his secret.

"I see dead people," Cole whispered. These visions are not figments of Cole's imagination. He explains to Dr. Crowe that he sees them when he is awake. They walk around like regular people. They only see what they want to see and they don't realize that they're dead. Cole lives in fear because he sees them wherever he goes. Though Dr. Crowe initially reasons Cole is delusional, he comes to believe that Cole possesses this special ability. Once he believes Cole, he is able to truly help him.

Dr. Crowe first helps Cole to understand that he is not a "freak," which is what others have labeled him. He explains that he is simply different and even special. He suggests to Cole that the people he sees need his help. This power of perception that is beyond Cole's five senses is actually a gift when viewed in the proper context. In order to use his gift, Cole must overcome his fear and insecurity and eschew the opinion of others. As Cole learns to understand the power of vision that he had been given, he is able to help others, including his mother and Dr. Crowe.

Cole's journey of self-discovery is not so different than that of a follower of Christ. As Paul wisely asserts in his first letter to the Corinthians, spiritual matters seem foolish to individuals that do not possess God's indwelling Spirit. This is because there are certain things in life that must be spiritually discerned. When we choose to follow Christ, we see the world from His perspective. We overcome our fear and most effectively navigate the road of life when we develop the power of perception referred to as spiritual vision.

Vision is the ability to see things differently. It is a God-given ability and in its highest form is activated by the Holy Spirit. While my definition of vision is simple, I believe the application is rare. This absence of vision results in frustration and discouragement; and because of it, many individuals are essentially lost on the road of life. Many people simply fail to realize the role that the Holy Spirit plays in our lives – particularly as it relates to spiritual vision. However, it is the insight provided through the revelation of God's Spirit that gives us our unique perspective and allows us to see our destination.

Impaired Vision

> *"Now we see things imperfectly as in a poor mirror, but then we will see everything with perfect clarity. All that I know now is partial and incomplete, but then I will know everything completely, just as God knows me now."*
> *1 Corinthians 13:12, NLT*

Just before their second missionary trip, Paul and Barnabas had a disagreement that caused them to part ways. John Mark, the nephew of Barnabas, unexpectedly abandoned the team during the first missionary trip. Paul opposed his inclusion on their second trip while Barnabas believed he should receive another chance. Unable or unwilling to resolve their dispute, the two men formed separate mission teams. Paul selected Silas as his chief companion and set out on a mission that would eventually take them to the European continent, including stops in Greece and Macedonia (part of modern-day Greece). The city of Corinth, located in southern Greece, was an important destination on Paul's second missionary trip. This was a return visit for Paul who had resided in Corinth for at least eighteen months during his first missionary trip.

During Paul's day, Corinth was a flourishing city with a population that was comparable to many modern-day cities. The city had a burgeoning upper class and the citizens were known for their wealth and luxury. Unfortunately, the citizens of Corinth were also known for their self-indulgence. The city had a notorious reputation for vulgarity and immorality. So much so that to live like a Corinthian was synonymous with drunkenness and recklessness. Given the city's reputation, it may seem curious that Paul spent so much time in Corinth. However, Paul had the uncommon ability to see other people and the world around him differently.

After another extended stay in Corinth, Paul continued his second missionary trip and eventually returned to his home base in Antioch. It was during his third missionary trip that Paul writes his first letter to the church at Corinth. Paul had received several disappointing reports concerning the assembly at Corinth. It seems that the Corinthian church was allowing their environment to influence them and not the other way around. The selfish and immoral behavior that citizens of Corinth were notorious for had crept into the local assembly. Paul was eager to get back to Corinth to address the fellowship personally. In the meantime, he penned a general letter to refocus his fellow journeymen on their ultimate destination.

It is a fundamental truth that how you see your destiny determines how you live your life. In this regard it can be said that the Corinthians suffered from impaired vision. Individuals who believe that they only have one life to live often engage in immoral and reckless behavior. Consciously or unconsciously, they reject the premise of eternal life and live only for the present.

Conversely, people who envision themselves ruling with Christ in His eternal kingdom act accordingly. These individuals conduct themselves on earth as God conducts Himself in heaven, believing that these two realities will be united in God's manifested kingdom.

In one powerful stanza of Paul's letter, he brings to light a paradox of the present world. He notes that while we have access to God's Spirit who imparts revelation, we still have a limited view of the road ahead. As Paul describes, we see things imperfectly. Everything we know about life is partial and incomplete. This reality should draw us closer to God – the source of all knowledge. Paul reminds his readers that when we arrive at our ultimate destination we will see things with perfect clarity. However, during our present lives we can't rely on our carnal understanding, which is often blurred by wayward emotions, unrighteous desires, or deceitful hearts. We must allow God to perfect our vision through the power of His Spirit.

A Different Point of View

If you're like me, you're asking yourself what practical implications proceed from these truths. If you accept that you have a God-ordained destination, you naturally must determine how you will get there. Vision is essential in this regard. While we ultimately have a common destiny, we know that no two paths are the same. Your path is exclusive to you and no one else will travel the road you tread. This is why you must learn to see the world differently. To acquire a *sixth sense*, so to speak. This unique perspective, made possible through the power of God's Spirit, enables you to make wise decisions when you come to those inevitable forks in the road.

When you make decisions, you must consider God's will as well as your unique personality and abilities. Successful travelers must learn to see themselves, their fellow travelers, and the world around them through the perspective that God gives them. It is only when you learn to view these three aspects of life from God's perspective that you will make decisions that will lead you to your destiny. This is an invaluable lesson that I am learning firsthand as God's Spirit enables me to navigate my own course.

Envisioning my destiny began with learning to see myself differently. I can honestly admit that I spent much of my adolescent and young adult life with an improper view of myself. I was very wary of the opinion of others and, like many people, I created a believable facade. I've since learned that if I don't look to God to affirm my identity and self-worth, I'm constrained by the opinions of other people. This is dangerous because identity is inextricably linked to destiny. As I've come to know God personally, I've learned to recognize and value my true self. While it is difficult to walk a mile in another person's shoes, it is impossible to fill their shoes for a lifetime. God has allowed me to uncover my true self, and I simply want to be the best me I can be.

Next, I had to learn to see others differently. When you have an improper image of self, you naturally have an improper perspective of others. This tainted view can manifest itself in many ways. Some people have a poor self-image, so they despise others. Some people are dishonest, so they mistrust others. Some people feel they are unlovable and have trouble loving others. In my case, I often sought affirmation from people. This often resulted in unrealistic expectations of people, expecting them to fill the void of a missing relationship with God. God's Spirit has enabled me to see myself and other people from His perspective. This vantage point allows me to develop healthy relationships with all types of people, loving them with the love of Christ.

Finally, God is teaching me to see the world around me differently. Growing up on the south side of Chicago, I spent most of my formative years within a few square miles. Early in our marriage, my wife and I committed to traveling to other parts of the world. Though we haven't traveled to every continent, we've visited parts of Europe, Africa, Asia, South America, Central America and the Caribbean. The opportunity to travel has opened my mind to new things and new possibilities that I would have never thought possible. God has expanded my spiritual perspective of the world in a similar way. Instead of problems, I see opportunities. Instead of suffering, I see salvation. I realize now that the reality of God's kingdom is greater than any temporal circumstance. With that mindset, I view each day as a wonderful gift from God.

Eyes on the Prize

It's a simple but profound truth that the closer you get, the clearer your destination becomes. This is how vision is linked to your ultimate destination. As God guides us through His Spirit and His Word, our obedience draws us closer to His kingdom. As we obey Him, we experience His love and faithfulness in new ways. Just as importantly, we come to know the surety of His Word. Things that seem unclear at the onset of our journey come into focus as we draw closer to God. Disobedience draws us away from God and in turn our ultimate destination. We become disoriented and confused because we lack focus and vision. Conversely, obedience to the Spirit's leading brings clarity to our decisions because our focus is clear.

The kingdom of God is at the same time a future and present reality. What does this mean? While we expectedly look forward to the physical manifestation of Christ's heavenly kingdom in the earth we also are admonished to think and act as kings in the present day. Recall that how you see your eternal life determines how you live in this present life. The kingdom of God represents Christ's rule in the earth through the hearts and lives of men and women. As joint heirs with Christ, we are charged with the responsibility to rule or govern the earth as God's representatives. All forms of government — including individual, family, civil, and church — are ordained and accountable to God.

When you make the kingdom of God your destination, you naturally adopt a kingdom mentality. This mentality is founded in humility and submission to the will of Christ, the King of kings. When we have this type of attitude, the Spirit of God intervenes in our lives. Jesus taught His disciples a valuable lesson with respect to application of the kingdom in the present life. He warned them that there would be those who would falsely claim the arrival of His manifested kingdom, saying it was one place or another. Jesus assured His followers that the kingdom of God was within them. The implication was that God's indwelling Spirit authorizes and enables mankind to rule in the earth as He does in heaven.

While reading an account of a mountain climber I was struck by a profound insight. The higher one climbs the more spectacular the view. Paradoxically, the higher one climbs the thinner the air and the more challenging the expedition. It occurred to me that this was a good metaphor for life's journey when guided by God's Spirit. Through faith, God leads us to higher heights. As we go from faith to faith, the summit comes closer into view. The closer we get to the summit or destination, the nearer we are to God. The journey challenges us, but it is a once-in-a-lifetime experience. As a man or woman of destiny, you must press toward the high place to which God is calling you. It is the perspective you gain from always looking up toward God that enables you to clearly see your destination.

•

Chapter

(4)

Have You Charted a Course?

"Stop fooling yourselves. If you think you are wise by this world's standards, you will have to become a fool so you can become wise by God's standards."
1 Corinthians 3:18, NLT

Early in my professional career, I learned an important life lesson regarding proper planning. Upon completing my graduate business degree, I was hired as an associate with an investment banking firm. My associate training program was very comprehensive, spanning nearly five months. While a large part of the training focused on honing key technical skills, the more important aspects were about immersing the associates in the corporate culture. Given that the organization was primarily organized in self-managed groups, self-awareness and team skills were essential for long-term success. The senior management of the firm contracted with Outward Bound to create a customized training module for our associate class.

Outward Bound is a non-profit organization that delivers active learning programs using unfamiliar settings to inspire self-discovery, character development, and teamwork. Their clients range from troubled teens to executives from Fortune 500 companies. The mission of Outward Bound is to help individuals and teams achieve their potential and effectively serve others. If you know anything about associate classes from investment banking firms, you can probably attest that the Outward Bound program was just the sort of experience that we needed. Translating personal ambition and achievement into teamwork and servant leadership was an important lesson for a group of over-caffeinated over-achievers.

Our excursion took us to a fairly remote part of upstate New York. We were divided into teams that cut across different areas of the firm, and thus we were unfamiliar with our teammates. We engaged in a full day of team-based activities that tested us physically and mentally. The culmination of the day of activities was a team competition. The competition was a mix between an obstacle course and a series of brain teasers. It required both physical prowess and mental dexterity. The course had five segments that could be completed in any order. The catch was that different members of the team had to complete different segments with the final segment being completed by the entire team.

The goal was clear and unambiguous: Complete the course before the other teams and be declared the victor. Having an action orientation, I was ready to get going. Though several of our team members were quite deliberate, the rest of us were confident we could figure things out on the fly. I was chief among this constituency. What followed was a comedy of errors as we managed to finish the course dead last. Though we naturally felt a need for urgency, the key to successfully and quickly finishing the course was proper planning. Had we taken time to chart our course, we would have discovered the most efficient ordering of the tasks and the most suitable individuals to assign to each task.

The Apostle Paul understood the value of planning. In his first letter to the Corinthians, he emphasizes wise planning based on godly standards. A casual review of Paul's travels lead some to incorrectly surmise that Paul went about his work with little or no planning. After all, isn't that what being led by the Spirit is all about? A closer study of Paul's missions reveals a very rational and disciplined approach. Although Paul was submissive to the leading of God's Spirit, he didn't shy away from developing a plan for his ministry and ultimately his life. While there were many unexpected occurrences during Paul's travels, Paul thoughtfully planned his missionary trips.

As with most things in life, there must be a balance. Paul tempered his rational disposition with spiritual disciplines that enabled him to be sensitive to the leading of God's Spirit. These disciplines included fasting, prayer, and meditation on the Word. Paul's first letter to the Corinthians also cautions us regarding the balance between our plans and God's purpose. We must not deceive ourselves by becoming wise in our own eyes. We accomplish this by seeking God's will concerning our plans. Paul readily adjusted His plans when the Holy Spirit directed him, demonstrating the practical reality of *driving under the influence.*

Like Paul, our dreams should be divinely inspired and our plans divinely endorsed. What big dream have you conjured up for your life? What great desire has God placed in your heart? What significant contribution to the human experience has captured your passion and creativity? Whatever the answer, I'm convinced of two things. First, you will need a carefully developed plan to realize your goal. Second, your plan must be aligned with God's purpose for your life if you want it to have lasting significance. Big dreams often languish or die due to a lack of prayerful planning.

All Roads Lead to Rome

"And the night following the Lord stood by him, and said,
Be of good cheer, Paul: for as thou hast testified of me in Jerusalem,
so must thou bear witness also at Rome."
Acts 23:11, KJV

A trusted assistant named Timothy became Paul's primary companion and co-worker on his third missionary trip. Paul articulated specific objectives including repeat visits to churches he'd previously established. I envision Paul painstakingly going over the itinerary for his third missionary trip with Timothy. Paul and Timothy would set out from Antioch for Macedonia and subsequently southern Greece visiting key assemblies along the way. Paul sent word ahead of their arrival of his desire to take up a collection from willing supporters. After delivering the collection to the church in Jerusalem, Paul had his heart set on going to Rome. Paul desired to preach the gospel in the city that was arguably the capital of the world at that time.

The Roman Empire was at the height of its influence and Rome was recognized by many as the preeminent city of the world. With a population of about three million, Rome was distinguished for great wealth, intellect, and culture. Paul was so committed to his plan to visit the Roman Church that he composed a letter informing them of his intentions. While Paul was eager to make his way to Rome, he did not stray from his planned stop in Jerusalem. A stopover in Jerusalem followed by a highly anticipated visit to Rome was his charted course. However, many of the best plans don't turn out quite as expected.

As Paul made his way to Jerusalem, he received several warnings of certain danger that awaited him in Jerusalem. Paul's companions urged him to change course and instead go directly to Rome. Nevertheless, Paul was determined to make his planned visit. Paul's travel plans came to an abrupt halt after he was accused of teaching practices and beliefs contrary to accepted Jewish tradition. Paul was attacked and beaten severely before eventually being imprisoned. I can picture a battered, bruised, and hungry Paul isolated in his cell. I suspect he was somewhat disheartened and may have become disillusioned concerning his plans. It was at this low point that the Spirit of God intervened.

Jesus appeared to Paul in a vision assuring him that he would indeed preach the gospel in Rome. How wonderful it must have been for Paul to have his plans confirmed by the Lord despite his circumstances. We should observe that Paul's road to Rome was not an easy one. The events that transpired in Jerusalem were followed by several years of trials and imprisonment. Paul, who was a Roman citizen, would eventually exercise his right to have his case tried before the Roman emperor. It was only then that Paul was transported to Rome where he preached the gospel before the emperor and other magistrates. What a powerful example this provides for us. If we align our plans with God's purpose, He will similarly direct our paths and confirm our plans.

Sounds Like a Plan

All other things being equal, we like to feel as though we're in control. Inasmuch as life is unpredictable by design, this puts our emotions at odds with our experience. Most people devise plans to help them manage the variability of life. Whether devising an educational plan, a career plan, or a financial plan, people generally engage in some level of planning. The spectrum ranges from those who do very limited planning to those who engage in meticulous planning. I admittedly fall into the latter category. For years I struggled to find the proper balance between my plans and God's purpose. After all, if God knows what He ultimately wants and is willing to direct my activities, isn't life mostly about listening?

The answer is simple but not easy. While the quality of our lives is directly related to our ability to hear from God, this in no way conflicts with the need for planning. In fact, I am convinced that God is actually pro-planning. What do I mean by that statement? The Bible encourages us to commit our pursuits to the Lord to ensure our plans are successful (Prov. 16:3). God is primarily concerned that we are focused on the right things. Therefore we should make seeking God part of our planning process. If our desires are righteous and our motives are pure, the Spirit will aid us in our planning. God places righteous desires in our hearts and fully expects that we will devise plans to realize them. All of us have this creative ability.

The purpose, or desired outcome, is the foundation of any sound plan. The Bible teaches us that though we may devise many plans, it is the Lord's purpose that will be established (Prov. 19:21). The indwelling Spirit reveals God's purpose and enables us to develop our plans into agreement. However, God does not stop there. The Spirit also aids us in the execution of our plans. The Bible teaches us that plans are devised in the mind, but the Lord directs our steps (Prov. 16:9). This does not mean that the Lord tells us every move we should make. As we mature we often require less direct intervention. It simply assures us that the Lord is standing ready to advise and encourage us. This is particularly true when we encounter life's inevitable tests and trials.

What Matters Most

We opened chapter 1 by highlighting the successful Volkswagen campaign that distinguished passengers from drivers. As we conclude the first section of the book, I'd like to highlight another brand campaign that I am personally familiar with. My current employer recently launched a comprehensive brand initiative. As a trusted advisor to successful organizations, families, and individuals, we provide customized fiduciary, banking, and asset management solutions. Our brand promise is to enable our clients to achieve the freedom to focus their time and energy on the things they deem most important. This is captured in our marketing campaign "the freedom to do what matters most." It is an ingenuous campaign and a powerful brand promise that resonates with our clients as well as the broader market.

As I reflected on the firm's brand promise, a more significant promise came to mind. Jesus promised His disciples that though He was departing to prepare a place for them that He would not leave them alone. He promised the aid of a comforter or counselor, which is the Holy Spirit. The Holy Spirit guided the disciples along the road of life and reminded them of the things Jesus taught them. The gift of the Holy Spirit is available to all who believe in Jesus Christ. As I considered our firm's brand promise alongside Jesus' promise to believers, a light bulb went on. The inner working of God's Spirit truly and completely frees us to do the things that matter most. That is the wonderful benefit that results from *driving under the influence* of the Holy Spirit.

God's purpose is eternal and supercedes our temporal plans or desires. When we accept God's counsel in the form of His Word, we are free from the bondage of sin, the opinions of others, and our own limited thinking. In short, we are free to live out the wonderful life that God has destined for us. It is God's destiny for our lives that matters most. And it is the Holy Spirit's influence on our plans that ultimately guides us to our destiny.

●

Part
2

Keep Your Motor Running

"Therefore, since we are surrounded by such a huge crowd of witnesses to the life of faith, let us strip off every weight that slows us down, especially the sin that so easily hinders our progress. And let us run with endurance the race that God has set before us. We do this by keeping our eyes on Jesus, on whom our faith depends from start to finish." Hebrews 12:1-2, NLT

Similar to Paul's first letter to the Corinthians, the author of Hebrews (also believed to be Paul) compares life's journey to a contest or race. We learned in the introduction of the first section that the crowning event of early athletic festivals was an endurance race. The concept of endurance is a recurring theme in Paul's letters. In describing life's journey, the author rightly acknowledges that God is the chief architect who sets our course before us. The author also provides wise counsel, which, if faithfully applied, will help us complete our journey.

The writer begins by focusing our attention on several men and women who led truly extraordinary lives as a result of their faith in God. These include the likes of Abraham, Sarah, Moses, Rahab, and Gideon. They serve as examples of individuals who successfully navigated the road that God set before them. The writer refers to these individuals as a multitude of witnesses surrounding or supporting us. Their testimonies serve as evidence that God's Spirit enables men and women to lead victorious lives. Our steadfast trust in God ensures us a place of equal prominence among the growing multitude of witnesses.

Next the writer admonishes us to lay aside every weight or encumbrance that might hinder our progress on the road of life. The primary encumbrance to progress during life's journey is sin, or disobedience to God. We briefly touched on this point in the second chapter of the text. Sin inhibits our relationship with God and thwarts His influence in our lives. Because God's presence and power are the necessary ingredients for a truly successful journey, we must separate ourselves from sin. Moreover, we must set aside any distractions that retard our progress in life. This includes seemingly innocent things that interfere with our relationship with God and His purpose for our lives. It is the discipline to set aside needless distractions and sin that makes us fit to complete our individual course.

Thirdly, the author touches on the quality of endurance or patience. The clear implication is that the *patient* competitor, as opposed to the most physically gifted, will endure to the end. The Greek word *hupomone*, which is translated endurance, involves both passive stamina and active perseverance. A patient competitor must have the fortitude to withstand the tests and trials of life and the determination to contest for the heavenly prize that awaits the victor. This type of endurance is achieved when human persistence is combined with the power of God's Spirit.

The author's final pearl of wisdom is priceless. The author reveals that the true determinant of success boils down to keeping our focus on Jesus Christ. Jesus' life epitomized what it means to finish. He is the owner and designer of the course and is the one in whom we must place our faith. It is the competitor who focuses on Christ's eternal kingdom as opposed to the temporal cares of this world who will successfully navigate the road of life.

If you've spent much time in an automobile, you've passed a stalled vehicle at one time or another. This is a fairly common sight for frequent travelers. Or, like me, perhaps you've had the experience of dealing with a stalled vehicle. I've required roadside assistance on more than one occasion, and I can personally attest that people don't begin a journey with the intention of stalling along the way. In fact, most drivers confidently assume they have the appropriate provision (fuel) and that they've undertaken the appropriate precautions (maintenance). Nevertheless, an unexpected breakdown teaches the humbling lesson that driving a car does not qualify you as a mechanic.

Intimate operating knowledge, proper maintenance, and adequate fuel are all required to successfully arrive at one's destination. In similar fashion, self-awareness, spiritual growth, and passion are required to successfully complete the journey of life. In section two of the text, we will turn our focus inward as we examine our attitude and our aptitude. We will examine the role that the Holy Spirit plays in teaching us about our unique design as well as our God-given abilities. We will also better understand how God's Spirit helps us avoid or recover from stalls along the way. It is the power and presence of the inner-working Spirit that keeps our motor running. As they say in NASCAR, start your engines!

●

Chapter

⑤

How Does Your Vehicle Operate?

"Live no longer as the ungodly do, for they are hopelessly confused.
Their closed minds are full of darkness; they are far away from the life of God
because they have shut their minds and hardened their hearts against him."
Ephesians 4:17b-18, NLT

During a recent business trip, I unwittingly enrolled in a refresher course in driver's education. My trip began with the all too familiar delayed flight. Needless to say, I was less than enthused when I finally arrived at my destination. Anxious to get to my hotel, I hurriedly placed my belongings in the rental car and headed for the freeway. I hadn't gotten five miles from the airport when I found myself in a sudden storm. As the rain beat violently against the windshield, I fumbled about in search of the controls for the wipers and the headlights. What should have been a straightforward operation proved surprisingly difficult given the circumstances.

After a tense moment, I sensibly pulled over to better familiarize myself with the controls. This experience actually taught me a valuable life lesson.

Even if an individual is confident in his or her destination, working knowledge of the means and method of travel is required. My failure to familiarize myself with the operation of the vehicle put me as well as other drivers in danger. Moreover, the objective of the journey itself was jeopardized.

It's easy to go through the motions in life. This is particularly true when we think we've got things figured out. Yet just as weather conditions can quickly change, so can the circumstances of life. It is often during adversity that our skillfulness or lack thereof is put to the test. We must tirelessly work to master the art of driving. Steering is not the same as driving. A driver must be able to maintain control of his or her vehicle in all types of conditions. It is only when the driver learns to master the operation of the vehicle that the driver can turn his or her attention to mastering the road.

In Paul's letter to the Ephesians, he warns his readers about the plight of the ungodly. Paul describes these travelers as hopelessly confused. To be clear, Paul's assessment has nothing to do with comprehension or intellect per se. Confusion is a direct result of closing one's mind to the instruction of God. Without the knowledge and wisdom of God, our minds are full of darkness and ignorance. In particular, we lack a clear understanding of our true identity and by extension the manner in which we operate.

Identity is oneness or sameness of essential character. In other words, the essence of who you are is found in God. Through our relationship with God our identity is established. We are created in the image of God, whose defining characteristic is holiness, which means set apart. Your true self is holy, set apart for God's use. This also means that your identity distinguishes you from others. This is why it is important to receive your affirmation from God your Father as opposed to other people. People will often attempt to label you. If you accept the opinion of others concerning your character, you have in effect rejected God's identity for you. When God made you, He actually destroyed the mold. Unlike people, God does not need to figure you out because He knew exactly what He desired when He birthed you into existence.

God is your creator and the source of your true identity. It is only when you submit to His Spirit that you discover your true identity. Through His Spirit, God reveals your purpose and the unique manner in which you operate. If you are to successfully reach your ultimate destiny, you must accept the sovereignty of God's will for your life. When you learn to operate in the way in which God designed you, it's glorious for others to behold. This is because no one else can function quite like you. God has distinctively designed you to adjust to the road that is set before you. In essence, your spiritual operating system is calibrated to navigate your individual course.

A New Attitude

"You were taught, with regard to your former way of life, to put off your old self, which is being corrupted by its deceitful desires; to be made new in the attitude of your minds; and to put on the new self, created to be like God in true righteousness and holiness." Ephesians 4:22-24, NIV

How do you operate? Your successful journey on the road of life depends on your understanding in this area. While you may share common characteristics or qualities with others, there is no one quite like you. Your eyes, teeth, fingerprints, and countless other physical attributes are distinct from every human being that has ever lived. Your psychological makeup is equally distinct and intricate. King David may have said it best when he declared that we are fearfully and wonderfully made. He went on to praise God for His marvelous handiwork (Ps. 139:14-15).

The manner in which you operate is in part a byproduct of your original design. By definition, your design dictates your operating procedures. Let me give you an example. If you are reading this book, it is most likely that you are in an environment that has a source of light. This is because your eyes require light in order to make out the images on the page. If it gets dark, you will either turn on a light or move to an environment where there is an available source of light. I don't have to witness your actions because I understand your design. And your design greatly influences how you operate.

This basic concept similarly applies to your psychological makeup. Your personality generally dictates how you behave or function in most circumstances. It also provides insight into your optimal operating conditions or preferred environment. Understanding your personality is essential for your family and professional relationships. Moreover, it is essential for finding your way on the road of life. And while I have an intellectual appreciation for the field of behavioral science and the practitioners thereof, I submit that the best source of insight into your personality comes from the one who designed you.

While we must ultimately look to God in the quest of self-discovery, behavioral scientists have articulated a fundamental framework that helps us explore our psychological design. This framework depicts the individual personality in two distinct parts. The core element is known as temperament or predisposition. The second element is known as character or disposition. Taken together, these elements of our personality determine how we act or react to the circumstances of life. Many of us struggle on the road of life because we haven't taken the time to thoroughly understand our personality. In turn we employ operating procedures that were never prescribed nor intended by our original designer. Let's explore these concepts in more detail.

Your temperament or predisposition refers to your natural tendency to act in a certain manner. It's what I like to refer to as your hardware. While this term is associated with behavioral science, I believe it is largely consistent with the way that God designs us. I like to think of it as a component of our spiritual DNA. Just as a genetic code predetermines our physical attributes, I believe that God predetermines the core elements of our psychological makeup. In a sense, God hardwires us for the purpose He has for our lives. In this respect I believe our temperament influences many of our interests, abilities, skills, and gifts.

Your character or disposition refers to an attitude of the mind that causes you to act in a certain manner. As such, your character is more often the result of nurture as opposed to nature. Your disposition is the product of the interaction between your temperament and your environment. This is why things such as religion, race, nationality, education, and socioeconomic status all influence your character. Inevitably, your character is whom you have chosen to be in light of the many influences in your life. Your character is the greatest single determinant of how you function given a specific set of circumstances. Moreover, character often becomes so ingrained that many of your actions occur subconsciously.

What does all of this have to do with your journey in life you might ask? Early in the text we established that God has predetermined our destination in life and is the choreographer of our journey. We subsequently established that we must function properly in order to persevere on the road of life. God seeks to influence our behavior and actions so that we successfully complete our course. One of the great paradoxes of life is that He can only accomplish this with our permission. Said another way, we must yield to His Spirit. In doing so, we learn how we optimally function and how we optimally interact with the world around us.

Your Starring Role

It may be helpful to think of life as a play. God is the screenwriter and director, and He has designated a role especially for you. No one can perform your role quite like you because it was written expressly for you. God wants nothing more than for you to assume the role, and you will never truly be happy unless you do. When you submit to the leading of God's Spirit, you are in essence saying to God that you are willing and ready to assume your role. You acknowledge Him as Lord – the director of the great play of life.

To truly appreciate this example, you have to appreciate certain things about the nature and character of God. God begins by writing the great play we know as the human experience. Remarkable though it may seem, He's already seen the ending in His mind's eye. This is why Isaiah could rightly declare that God declares (writes) the end in the beginning and then allows His play to unfold (Isa. 46:10). With the end in mind, God introduces you to the action at a preferred place and preferred time to carry out a preferred role. By that I do not mean to imply that every action of your life is scripted. I simply mean to imply that you are especially chosen to make a contribution to this generation. As such, your race, ethnicity, nationality, socioeconomic status, and every other criterion that were circumstances of your birth are not a mistake. They are a deliberate choice by God your Creator.

God fully knows the circumstances He births us into and, in turn, gives us a temperament that best accommodates His purpose for our lives and the road we must navigate. Nevertheless, we ultimately have the freedom of choice and must choose whether we will assume the role He has designated for us. This is where the element of character or disposition comes into play. Recall that our character is who we ultimately choose to be. Though unique, our character is meant to display the character traits of God. This is why the Bible gives us so much insight into God's character or nature. The Word of God and Spirit of God are meant to be the dominant influences in our lives, overwriting any unlicensed software and enabling us to glorify God through our lives.

Mistaken Identity

Though God has written a starring role for each of us, the stark reality is that most people fail to assume their role. Your personal destiny can be viewed as the role God specifically envisioned for you. This is why we must understand God's eternal plan, which gives purpose to our individual lives. We must learn to accept God's will (role) for our lives and not rely on our limited understanding or selfish ambition. Failure to submit to His Spirit invariably results in a case of mistaken identity — the effects of which can be harmful and even fatal.

Humankind has been quietly and subtly engulfed in a widespread identity crisis. It began with Adam and Eve and continues to escalate to this day. Simply observe the world around you. Media and advertisement were once the byproduct of our lifestyle. Now media and advertisement are more likely to dictate our lifestyle. Adolescents regularly adopt behaviors and character traits of individuals they idolize rather than the unique character that God has ordained for them. Middle aged men and women suffer crisis when they wake up to the realization that their lives have been dictated by others and not ordained by God. They never understood who God intended them to be and they're unhappy with the person they've become.

The epidemic of mistaken identity has little to do with religion per se. Local churches, synagogues, and mosques are full of individuals who don't know their true identity. The problem has a spiritual origin and not a religious origin. I don't make this observation in a judgmental way. My personal and religious experiences have taught me that this is one of the most difficult questions that we face. Local churches, for example, often have a clear understanding of corporate vision and God's purpose for the body of Christ. Most believers can identify with seeking and saving the lost (having been lost themselves). Many have even matured to the level of understanding Christ's admonishment to seek, establish, and expand His kingdom. While our collective purpose and identity as the church is often clear, our individual identities often remain unclear.

I can personally attest to this truth because I spent much of my life assuming a character that God never intended for me. In doing so, I assumed behaviors and attitudes that were inconsistent with God's purpose for my life. I was simply out of character. Maybe you've had a similar experience. Maybe you feel like you are not quite in the space that God intends for you. It is important to note that this is not so much a distinction of moral values or religious practice. You can be a morally good person and not know God. You can be a religious person living a biblically based lifestyle and still fail to fulfill the purpose that God intends for you. Purpose is tied to identity and identity is about being one with God's Spirit.

I'm going to say something that you may find uncomfortable, but try it on for size. You may not be who you think you are. Thus you may not be fully operating in the space and the manner that God intended for you. I believe that most of us must stare down this reality at some point or another during our natural lives. The sad part is that pride will often blind us to this truth; like the adage says, ignorance is bliss. Success in life cannot and must not be measured by human standards. Our inclination to do so is a large contributor to the epidemic of mistaken identity. We must dismiss the notion of living a "good" life as measured by others. As one writer profoundly observed, satisfaction with "good" results often hinders our ability to achieve "great" results. Similarly, a "good" life often distracts us from a "God-ordained" life.

If you accept that you've been out of character, you must similarly accept that you have not been operating in the manner God intended. If you want to understand how you should operate, you must examine yourself from God's perspective. You must expel any attitude that is inconsistent with God's Word. You must adopt the character traits of God and begin to act like Him. You can not simply submit in those areas that are convenient for you, rather you must submit in every area of your life as God reveals your need for change. Only then will you understand how to function properly. Only then will you be qualified to exercise spiritual gifts and effectively serve others.

The Apostle Paul understood this process. I think this is why approximately eleven years passed before Paul set out on his missionary journeys. He needed to be taught by the Holy Spirit. That education was not so much about his knowledge of scripture, because he was a teacher of the law. It was not so much about determining his assignment, because that was communicated to him early on. The Holy Spirit revealed God's sovereign plan for mankind and more specifically the role God intended for Paul to play. This required Paul to discover his true identity and involved both learning and unlearning a great many things.

Having personally traveled the road to self-discovery, Paul could admonish the believers in Ephesus as they traveled a similar path. Paul admonished them to set aside the old self-image born out of misguided ambitions and desires. Paul encouraged them to take on their true identity, which was created righteous and distinct in the image of God. The new attitude of the mind that Paul described is the key to functioning as God intended. Like these early believers, we too must be taught to see ourselves through the eyes of God so that we can operate the way that He intends. This perspective is only achieved when we submit to the leading of His Spirit.

•

6

Have You Checked Under the Hood?

"Be careful then, dear brothers and sisters. Make sure that your own hearts
are not evil and unbelieving, turning you away from the living God.
You must warn each other every day, as long as it is called 'today,'
so that none of you will be deceived by sin and hardened against God."
Hebrews 3:12-13, NLT

Earlier in the text I shared an anecdote about my first automobile. My beloved 1983 Oldsmobile Omega was the source of several important life lessons. One such lesson occurred during the summer between my freshman and sophomore years of college. I'd returned to Chicago to work during the summer. Just prior to my return to school, a hose to the radiator burst, causing the engine to overheat due to the loss of coolant. My knowledge of automobiles was neither wide nor deep, but the problem seemed to have an obvious solution. With the help of my father (who actually knows a thing or two about automobiles), I replaced the busted hose and replenished the coolant. A week later, I was on the road making the thousand-mile drive to Tallahassee, Florida.

Since I was driving alone I decided to follow the family of a close friend who was also headed down to school. We set out on a Saturday evening expecting to make it to our destination by mid day on Sunday. About ten hours into the trip I witnessed the first sign of trouble — the dreaded engine light. The indicator is there to inform the driver that something has gone wrong, but it was the last thing I wanted to see ten hours into a seventeen-hour trip. I hoped it was an anomaly and continued for the time being. Two hours later it became apparent that I was in trouble. The engine began to stall and while I could ignore the engine light, the laboring engine could not be ignored. Our traveling party pulled off the interstate to evaluate the situation. When I popped the hood, the white puffs of smoke affirmed the earlier signals.

We were in a small town in Alabama on a Sunday, so just about everything was closed. We made our way to a service station where they were kind enough to call in an off-duty mechanic. After several hours, the mechanic arrived. He performed several diagnostic tests and discovered that my thermostat needed to be replaced. The good news was it could be repaired immediately. The bad news was that the repair would cost me a princely sum given my meager college budget. Three hours later and three hundred dollars poorer, I was back on the road to my destination.

When I arrived at school, I phoned my father to tell him about the incident. While he was happy to know I'd arrived safely, he shared with me an interesting fact about the repair. He explained to me that the thermostat for my vehicle cost less than ten dollars and took about five minutes to replace. Although I was appreciative of the southern hospitality I'd received, I realized that the service was relatively expensive. I actually wasn't upset with the mechanic because I realized the root cause of the problem. The thermostat had been damaged when my radiator hose burst prior to leaving Chicago. My failure to do a thorough diagnostic check of the engine resulted in my unexpected delay and costly lesson.

While preparing to write this book, I pondered how I've similarly moved through periods in my life without checking under the hood. By that I mean that I failed to thoroughly examine my inclination, motives, or reasoning for specific courses of action. Similar to the automobile example, things generally appear fine to both the individual and the outside world. The truth is that there are problems brewing on the inside. As is the nature of problems, they are eventually manifested on the outside.

The writer of Hebrews presciently identifies the source of many problems as the human heart. The writer admonishes his readers to check under the hood so to speak. He warns that undetected sickness of the heart causes us to turn away from God. This is a dangerous state of affairs because any time that we are heading away from God we are most assuredly heading in the wrong direction. Like engine trouble, a troubled heart jeopardizes our journey along the road of life. This is why we need God's indwelling Spirit to search the deep chambers of our heart.

Heart and Soul

"For the word of God is quick, and powerful, and sharper than any two-edged sword, piercing even to the dividing asunder of soul and spirit, and of the joints and marrow, and is a discerner of the thoughts and intents of the heart."
Hebrews 4:12, KJV

The human being is an intricate creation. The Bible tells us that when God created man, He introduced His Spirit or life force into the body that He had formed from the earth. The name Adam literally means dark or red earth. When God's life force entered into the body that He had formed, the man became a living soul. As such, the human construct has three components. The body is the physical part of the human construct, which was formed to live in and interact with the earth. The spirit is the part of our being that is from God and relates to God. The soul or inner man is the essence of who we are.

The heart and the mind are the two essential parts of the soul. These two members mirror the physical organs that are vital to our natural lives. For example, the brain is the command center of our physical bodies. And just as the brain gives vital instructions to the body, the mind must skillfully captain the soul. When referring to our intellectual capacity, the New Testament of the Bible often uses the Greek word *nous*, which we translate to the English word *mind*. The mind is the seat of reflective consciousness. It houses the faculties that enable us to perceive, judge, and determine. In short, the mind is the part of our being where decisions are ultimately made.

Our physical heart is like an engine that fuels the body with life. Just as the physical heart pumps life-sustaining blood through our natural body, the spiritual heart is designed to store and disperse the life-sustaining Word of God in the inner man. The term *heart* is defined as the inner part of a person or thing. The New Testament of the Bible regularly uses the Greek word *cardia*, which we translate *heart*. This is also where we derive the English word *cardiac*. The heart is the seat of our subconsciousness. While closely linked to the mind, the heart serves a distinct function. It is the repository where we store things such as inclinations, desires, and emotions. Morality and creativity are actually a function of the heart.

The heart and the mind are inextricably linked by the manner in which our soul functions. Our most frequent and essential activity is that of making decisions. We may make thousands of them in a typical day. The mind is the place where we process inputs that drive our decisions. The heart is the primary contributor of those inputs. For example, have you ever noticed that you have relatively predictable responses to certain requests or external stimuli? This is in part because your predisposition encodes certain inclinations in your heart. Subconsciously, or "without thinking" as we sheepishly say, we respond in predisposed ways. The reality is that we have made a decision based on inputs stored in our heart.

Soul System

As I've pondered the symbiotic relationship between the heart and the mind, I've come to think that the interaction is like that of the central processing unit (CPU) of a computer. The mind functions like the operating software of the CPU. The operating software performs the necessary tasks of deciphering inputs and instructions, keeping track of the data and programs stored on the hardware, and controlling the peripheral devices. The hardware or memory is where vital programs and data are stored, filed, and accessed. So, if the operating software makes the decisions, the memory provides the basis or inputs whereby the decisions are made.

In considering the purpose and function of the heart, I've realized that it is the part of our being that God designed in order to influence us. God begins this process long before we realize. God told the prophet Jeremiah that before he was conceived that He knew or created him. He goes on to tell Jeremiah that He fashioned him while he was in his mother's womb (Jer. 1:5). I believe that God hardwires us such that we are inclined to respond in certain ways. This hardwiring affects our interests, desires, and motivations. It is in part what contributes to what behavioral scientists refer to as our predisposition. Like Jeremiah, we are all carefully fashioned and equipped for the assignments that God intends for us.

God also seeks to influence our character or disposition once we are born. Recall from chapter 5 that our character or disposition is who we choose to become. God's primary means of influencing our actions is through His Word. Worship and prayer are also essential activities. It is through fellowship with God that we learn His will concerning us and His instructions for our lives. King David was distinguished by God as being an individual who knew His heart. This is because David spent time in fellowship with God. In Psalm 119 King David declared that he'd stored God's Word in his heart so that he would not stray from the course that God had set him on. Similarly, God desires each of us to seek His counsel and store His words in our heart.

The mind and the heart work so seamlessly that it is difficult to distinguish the two. For example, there are thoughts of the mind, which we might refer to as reasoning. Alternatively, there are thoughts of the heart, and we might refer to those as meditation. Our heart stores the things we meditate on and they become part of our subconscious self. Our meditations affect our self-image and help shape our worldview. The quality of our lives is determined by our decisions, and our decisions are in large part a function of the condition of our heart. This is why many of us fall into the trap of repeating bad behavior or decisions. We fail to examine the source, which is often the things we have stored in our heart.

Heart Attack

Our society, culture, family, friends, and even our adversary the devil all have the ability to affect the condition of our hearts. For that reason we must be careful of the things that we allow to pass by our five senses and reach our hearts. The Bible gives us clear instruction in this area when it instructs us to guard our hearts with all diligence because it influences everything we do (Prov. 4:23). Anything that we allow to reside in our heart influences who we are and the decisions we make. This is why we must be circumspect of the things we listen to, the things we view, and the company we keep. Our failure to appreciate the nature and function of the heart renders us defenseless against negative outside influences that jeopardize our journey.

Recall our earlier analogy comparing the soul to the central processing unit of a computer system. The concept of protecting a computer's hardware against viruses is akin to the concept of guarding our heart. A virus is a code or program that loads itself onto a computer without the user's knowledge. A virus can damage important files stored in the memory, disrupt normal operation, or disable the system altogether. The effects of most viruses are subtle inasmuch as they perform undetected operations. They often do just enough to impair performance but not enough to make the user fully aware of their presence.

Just as computers are commonplace, so too are the antivirus software programs that are employed to protect them. As I sit here at my computer pouring over the words in this chapter, my system is being protected by antivirus software. The software is designed to detect unwanted programs that attempt to infiltrate my system and take up residence on my hardware. The programs are also designed to detect unusual activity that I may be unaware of. The antivirus program not only warns me of unwelcome activity but with my permission will prohibit access and remove uninvited programs. In short, the antivirus software guards my system's heart.

The Holy Spirit serves a similar function when we give Him permission to search our hearts. As we noted earlier in the chapter, it is impossible to effectively search one's heart without the assistance of God's Spirit. God's Word is the standard by which we must judge all things. This is why the Holy Spirit assists us by revealing the truth of God's Word. Paul notes that God's Word is so powerful that it allows us to clearly distinguish the spirit from the soul. Said another way, it distinguishes God's will from our selfish desires. Paul goes on to teach us that the word of God allows us to judge the thoughts and attitudes of the heart.

Matters of the Heart

Maybe you are suffering from loneliness because your heart is sick and you have a distorted view of yourself. You don't see yourself as attractive and that is the image you portray to others. You accept less than you deserve because you don't see the beauty God sees when He looks at you — the same beauty He envisioned when He created you. Maybe you have a troubled marriage. Your heart is sick, which impairs the way you view your marriage and your mate. You're not able to love your mate the way the Bible teaches because you haven't changed the way that you see him or her. You have not changed the way that you see your spouse because you are unaware of the need of a change of heart.

Maybe you've become distant or even estranged from family and friends. Maybe you don't communicate well with others. You're not a bad person. The truth is quite contrary. Nonetheless, you've picked up bad habits along the course of your life. You've accepted a false image of yourself. This condition of the heart alters the way you view those around you and, more importantly, the way you view yourself. Whether you are dealing with these types of situations or other similar ones, deliverance can only come as a result of a changed heart.

While change is both necessary and rewarding, it is also hard work. Certain changes we must make are even painful. This is why many people spend their lives conforming and never truly changing. The desire to change and the ability for change are birthed out of the proper self-image. We are created in the image and likeness of God. Through His Spirit, God reveals all that He is and all that we are meant to be. It is this glorious revelation that makes the perfecting process of personal change worth the work.

I can personally attest to the need for self-examination. One such occasion in my own life occurred several years ago. The business that I'd started with a partner was struggling financially, which resulted in a fair amount of anxiety. The Holy Spirit revealed that anxiety was not the problem, rather it was a symptom. The root cause of my anxiety was a lack of faith, which adversely impacted my perspective as well as my actions. Instead of seeking God for answers, I relied on my own understanding. My perceived problems were looming larger than God's promises. Through the power of God's Word,

I allowed the Holy Spirit to search my heart. This helped me to identify the unhealthy attitudes that I needed to change. This practical experience of checking under the hood was the genesis for my previous book, *Ridiculous Faith*.

In the preceding chapter, we highlighted the importance of understanding how we function. We determined that a Christ-like attitude is the key to functioning properly. It is equally essential that we regularly check under the hood, or examine ourselves. This regular maintenance ensures that we have not internalized anything that is inconsistent with God's will for our lives, which, in turn, would compromise our ability to function properly. In the same way that we solicit the expertise of a mechanic to run diagnostic tests on our automobile, we need the revelation of the Holy Spirit to effectively examine our hearts. With regular checkups, we can be assured that our heart will properly serve us along the ever-changing road of life.

•

⑦

What Special Features Do You Have?

"Now there are varieties of gifts, but the same Spirit.
And there are varieties of ministries, and the same Lord.
There are varieties of effects, but the same God who works all things
in all persons. But to each one is given the manifestation
of the Spirit for the common good."
1 Corinthians 12:7:4-7, NIV

There are certain experiences in life that are more memorable than others. Events such as your high school senior prom, your wedding day, or the birth of your children mark key chapters in your life. First-time experiences, whether sentimental or mundane, are often stored as vivid memories. Most people can readily recall their first day of school, first kiss, or first day on the job. One such experience for me was the first time my wife and I purchased a new car. Anyone who has purchased a new car can attest to the pain and pleasure of this memorable experience.

My wife and I had been married for just over a year. My beloved 1983 Oldsmobile Omega had been retired for several years. My preferred mode of transportation was Chicago's commuter transit system. My wife, also a commuter, owned a 1984 Toyota Corolla. The small grey warrior was the first car she'd ever owned. The car had migrated north from Florida to Chicago when my wife made the move. The previous owner had covered one hundred thousand miles of open road in the Corolla and my wife had dutifully added another fifty thousand miles during her stewardship.

My wife has always been thrifty. She'd managed to retire her graduate school debt within two years of completing her MBA. After a good deal of research and persuasion, I convinced her to purchase a new car. Rightly or wrongly, I viewed it as a just reward for her discipline and hard work. One Friday evening we climbed into the Corolla and made our sojourn to an automobile dealership we'd identified on the Internet. If you're a city dweller, you'll understand that we ventured to what seemed like the outskirts of civilization to reach the suburban dealership.

For two individuals who'd never owned a new automobile (or one built during that decade), the dealership was a revealing experience. The new automobiles performed the same basic function as our current automobile – transport from point to point. However, the functionality of the newer models in concert with the numerous special features made the driving experiences quite distinctive. Power locks and windows, heated seats and mirrors, and a multidisc CD changer may sound very passé given today's sophisticated vehicles, but this was a serious upgrade from what we were accustomed to. The packages of options were unique and the permutations from which a buyer could choose seemed endless.

After a withering round of negotiations (which I suspected were artificially prolonged), my wife settled on a fully loaded four-door sedan. She parted ways with her faithful Corolla and joined the legions of new car owners on the road. The early weeks of our new car experience were a bit amusing. We literally had more features than we could handle. Like most car buyers, we didn't quite view the owner's manual as required reading. But when the stereo inexplicably shut off, we decided to adopt a novel approach and actually read the owners manual. After a little reading and a lot of experience, we adjusted to our increased functionality and numerous features.

Maybe you've never thought of it this way, but on the road of life we are very much like sophisticated vehicles. God intricately designs us for a common experience, yet we each are endowed with a unique set of tools or talents. While we all have the capacity to reach our ultimate destination, our journey's success is greatly affected by the way we use our talents. As my wife and I learned, a driver must skillfully utilize the automobile's special features in order to fully maximize the driving experience. Likewise a fulfilling journey on the road of life depends in part on your willingness to develop and deploy your God-given talents.

The Apostle Paul addresses this matter in a letter to believers at Corinth. He explains that God endows each of us with unique talents. When we allow God to direct our efforts as we serve others, His Spirit endows us with power. We refer to these God-given talents as spiritual gifts because we operate in such a way that our service benefits others. Paul further explained that although our talents are diverse, God is the source of them all. His Spirit not only imparts talents but imbues us with power so the gifts are profitable for the common good. The special talents we receive from our maker equip us for life's journey. They are a means to provide for ourselves, serve others, and glorify God. Our unique set of talents also helps create a distinctive experience along life's winding road.

Fully Equipped

> *"It is the one and only Holy Spirit who distributes these gifts.*
> *He alone decides which gift each person should have."*
> 1 Corinthians 12:11, NLT

My father is fond of saying that God equips us for the purpose for which He sends us. His instruction has always been the foundation for my understanding in the area of spiritual gifts. In chapter 5 we discussed the manner in which we operate. We established that God specially designed each of us so that we can navigate our individual course. Understanding the way we are designed to operate helps ensure a successful journey in life. Similarly, we must identify the special talents that God has given to us and master their use. Our God-given talents provide insight into God's plan for our lives as well as the means to accomplish these plans.

Earlier in the chapter we noted that each of us has a unique set of talents that we can develop and employ. For ease of understanding I generally use two broad categories to classify these talents. The first category is what I refer to as abilities. I define ability as an innate talent or aptitude. These are areas where we are naturally proficient. Examples may include artistic ability, problem solving, communication skills, athleticism, and the like. Ability may be a function of your personality or more specifically the predisposition God has given you. Ability may also be a function of your heritage in the sense that it is genetically or culturally passed down.

The second broad category is what I refer to as skills. I define a skill as a learned proficiency. In this respect it is more of an acquired expertise. Skills are generally developed as a result of education or training. In essence they are competencies that we are taught and then master through application and practice. Many of our professional vocations are acquired skills. For example, we may develop skills in interpreting law, repairing automobiles, styling hair, or providing financial advice. While we must develop our abilities and skills, there is a subtle but important distinction in my mind. Abilities tend to be more a function of nature or predisposition. Skills tend to be more a function of nurture or training.

This discussion then brings us to the concept of spiritual gifts. Paul's letter to the Corinthians takes great care to deal with the concept of spiritual gifts. These special talents were described by Paul as diverse endowments that were distributed and operated by God's Spirit. Paul noted that the concept of spiritual gifts was a source of misunderstanding and division during his time. I believe this is true even today. Nonetheless, I believe if we accept the basic tenets of the Bible and avoid the tendency to add to them, we can have a clear understanding of this concept. Moreover, we can learn how God's Spirit can work through us utilizing our God-given talents.

The term *gift* is translated from the Greek word *charisma*, which means grace. As such, a spiritual gift is an endowment of God's grace or power through the inner working of the Holy Spirit. When we submit to His influence, God empowers us to function in certain capacities that benefit the body of believers known as the church. By extension, these same spiritual gifts benefit other individuals whom we come in contact with.

Along for the Ride

As I delved further into scripture seeking practical insight regarding spiritual gifts, I revisited a promise Jesus made to His disciples at the end of His earthly ministry. Jesus told His followers that although He was departing that He would not leave them alone or powerless. He instead promised them that He would send them another *Comforter* (John 14:16). The *Comforter*, or Holy Spirit, would pick up where Jesus left off by guiding and empowering His disciples. The term *Comforter* is only used on four occasions in the New Testament. Each occasion is found in the gospel of John and in every instance it is Jesus who is speaking. The term *Comforter* is translated from the Greek Word *parakletos*, which means advocate, helper, or assistant. I believe Jesus' choice of words gives us great insight into the work of the Holy Spirit as well as the application of spiritual gifts.

Each of us has God-given talents that we can develop and deploy. When we enjoy a personal relationship with God, His Spirit works alongside us for the common good. In a manner of speaking, the Holy Spirit accompanies us on the road of life. While God empowers us, it is important to understand that He does not do all of the work for us. It is our responsibility to identify our innate abilities, acquire useful skills, and become proficient in our talents and skills. Moreover, it is our responsibility to seek the will of God with respect to how we use our talents. God's Spirit picks up where our human ability tapers off. So while a person may have great natural abilities or impressive acquired skills, it is the influence of God that makes the difference. When we accept God's will for our lives and make the conscious decision to follow Christ, God helps us to most effectively put our abilities and skills to use.

When our ability (whether it is innate or acquired) is married with the power of God's Spirit, the product is referred to as a spiritual gift. God's grace enhances our abilities and skills, enabling us to effectively serve others. Although people are quick to refer to talented individuals as anointed by God or blessed with a spiritual gift, we must be circumspect in this area.

The Bible cautions us that evil men can appear to be ministers of God if we mistake performance for power (2 Cor. 11:15). As Paul ascertained, spiritual gifts are distributed and operated by God's Spirit. Therefore it is only when God is in control that spiritual gifts are in operation. When we put spiritual gifts in the proper perspective, we understand Paul's admonishment to his protégé Timothy whom he admonished to actively deploy the gift God had given him (2 Tim. 1:6). The gift Paul was referring to is the grace or power of the Holy Spirit. We must likewise seek to actively serve others by becoming connected with God's Spirit and doing His will.

What He Loves About You

What special abilities or skills has God blessed you with? Are you using these talents to benefit others and to glorify God? These are critically important questions because they are intimately tied to your purpose here on earth. Recall that God had something specific in mind when he created you. Regardless of what you may have been told, your life is by no means an accident. God knows you and He knows the capacity that He placed in you. You must allow the Holy Spirit to develop your God-given abilities and skills. Your mastery of your talents will enrich your life as well as the lives of the countless people you touch.

Paul's letter also teaches us that God alone determines what spiritual gifts operate in our lives. The same God predisposes us to certain behaviors, births us into specific circumstances, and blesses us with certain innate abilities. This is why we should not covet the talents, possessions, or heritage of others. God has furnished us with exactly the equipment we need to complete our journey. We should therefore focus our attention and efforts on mastering the tools that God has given us. No one else is quite like you, and by extension no one can deploy your set of talents the way that you do. The distribution of spiritual gifts further emphasizes God's love of diversity.

God's thoughts are far superior to our own. For example, God's answer to the debate about equality is the proliferation of diversity. God has made us all wonderfully different. That's what He loves about us. He accentuates our beauty by giving us differing abilities and skills. When we operate under the leading of His Spirit, we deploy these talents in a manner that is unique.

Paul explained God's intent by describing believers as members of one body. The body is a unit made up of many distinct parts. The parts serve different purposes but work together for the benefit of the whole. At our finest, that is what God expects of the human family. Each member is charged with the responsibility to deploy his or her talents in unique ways but working toward the common good. This type of unity is only achieved when we follow the leading of God's Spirit.

I remember coming to the personal realization that God has blessed me with certain abilities. They include teaching, writing, problem solving, coordination, and diplomacy. Looking back over my life I can see that these abilities were prevalent at a very early age. Those innate abilities require cultivation as well as the guidance of God's Spirit. As I have grown closer to God, I've learned to appreciate the way that God has designed me and my abilities. Along the way, I have also developed certain skills that can be used for His glory. It is a simple truth that I am most fulfilled when I am employing my talents to serve others and glorify God. This underscores the fact that our gifts are ultimately for the benefit of others. After all, isn't sharing with others what gift giving is all about?

Maybe you are seeking God in order to uncover the talents He has blessed you with. Maybe you have a clear understanding of your talents and you are seeking His guidance as you develop and deploy those talents. Whatever the case, God rewards those who diligently seek Him. God constantly searches for those whom He can display His might through. I pray that you will allow God to perfect you and that your special features will shine brightly. Your special features are important tools that God uses to help guide you down the road of life.

●

Chapter

8

Have You Filled Up Your Tank?

"I pray that from his glorious, unlimited resources he will give you
mighty inner strength through his Holy Spirit. And I pray that Christ
will be more and more at home in your hearts as you trust in him.
May your roots go down deep into the soil of God's marvelous love.
And may you have the power to understand, as all God's people should,
how wide, how long, how high, and how deep his love really is.
May you experience the love of Christ, though it is so great you will
never fully understand it. Then you will be filled with the fullness of life
and power that comes from God."
Ephesians 3:16-19, NLT

If you spent your adolescent years during the early eighties or you happened
to be the parent of an adolescent during that time, you're likely familiar with
the rise of the rap music genre. Whether fan or foe, hardly anyone will argue
that rap music has been nothing short of a cultural phenomenon. James
Todd Smith III, more commonly known as LL Cool J, is one of the most

widely recognized names in the business. Though Mr. Smith is not counted among the creators of the genre, he is considered one of its pioneers and his career has spanned nearly three decades. Music aficionados credit Mr. Smith and others of his ilk with the migration of rap music from the urban underground to the cultural mainstream.

During the summer of 1987 the popularity of rap music was rising with the summer heat. At that time, rap music was primarily the province of urban youth. The purveyors of the trade, mostly male, were generally perceived as tough and street savvy. As one might imagine, there was no lack of bravado in the vainglorious anthems. The boasting over beats reinforced the stereotypical images of the performers. It was to this backdrop that Mr. Smith released the first commercially successful "rap ballad." Now if you're thinking that the term "rap ballad" is an oxymoron, your position is understandable. Nonetheless, Mr. Smith confessed to anyone who would listen that his love tank was essentially empty.

It is interesting to note that the first track on Mr. Smith's sophomore album was immodestly titled "I'm Bad." It's four-and-a-half minutes of nonstop machismo. Nevertheless, eight songs later Mr. Smith is shamelessly admitting his need for love. "I Need Love" was not only a commercial success, but it was a groundbreaking effort. The song quickly became popularized among nontraditional fans of the genre. And while many laud the creativity of the producers, I believe there was something less obvious at work. It might be hard for some to buy my argument, but I believe the song echoed a poetic truth that resonated with many listeners. Even the toughest people long to be loved. Deep down isn't that what we're all really after? To be fair, Mr. Smith was specifically referring to romantic love. And lest I get carried away, it was just a rap song. However, if you look hard enough you can find truth in some unlikely places.

The song depicts Mr. Smith carelessly careening along the road of life. His lyrics belie the musings of a nineteen-year-old who has much to learn about love and life. Mr. Smith's joyride takes an unexpected turn when he begins to lose interest in his juvenile pursuits. The story crescendos as he realizes for the first time in his life that he longs to be loved. He figuratively runs out of gas; or, better stated, he realizes that his love tank was empty all along.

Though unlikely his primary objective, Mr. Smith's lyrics reveal a fundamental truth about life's journey. Love is unquestionably our greatest emotional need. On the road of life, love is the fuel that keeps us forging ahead. When Jesus was asked about the greatest commandment, He quickly replied that we should love God with our whole heart. Incidentally, a close second was that we should love others the way we love ourselves (Mark 12:30-31). Have you ever considered that God requires love and so do we? Without love, it is impossible to successfully complete life's journey. Love defines our relationship with God, and it is mutual love that draws us toward God and in turn our destiny.

Inasmuch as art often imitates real life, I can personally relate to the experience of running out of gas. I was a couple of years out of college and things couldn't have been better... on the outside anyway. I was living in New York City and working for a prestigious Wall Street firm. I'd decided to pursue a graduate degree in finance and had recently been accepted to my first choice, the University of Chicago's Booth School of Business. I'd literally and figuratively covered a lot of distance since my childhood days on the Southside of Chicago. To top it all off, I was engaged to marry my college sweetheart later that year. I didn't think I was longing for love, but, like Mr. Smith, I simply didn't realize it.

Although there were a number of positive things happening in my life, I had a growing uneasiness on the inside. During my teenage years, I had forsaken my faith and begun to live in a manner that severed my relationship with God. I didn't live a reckless lifestyle. However, I knew that many of my decisions had put me in direct opposition to God's will for my life. I neither felt the presence nor the influence of God in my life. I realized that the uneasiness that I felt was something more critical. I found myself on the road of life driving with an empty tank.

When the true condition of my heart was revealed, it hit me like a head-on collision. Although I enjoyed healthy loving relationships with family, friends, and fiancé, I'd turned my back on the greatest love of all. And though I tried to tell myself otherwise, I couldn't fully love myself or others if I couldn't love God. Truth is a powerful and liberating force if we choose to accept it. Accepting the truth that I desperately needed God's love turned my emptiness into brokenness. By this I mean a broken and contrite sprit as opposed to a broken heart. This created a thirst for God's righteousness that has captured me in an entirely new love affair.

The Power of Love

In his letter to believers at Ephesus, the Apostle Paul went to great lengths to stress the power of God's love. Paul assures his fellow journeymen of God's unlimited spiritual resources. Paul indeed prays that his readers will draw from the inner reservoir of strength that is available through the work of God's Spirit. Moreover, Paul directly links the resources or inner strength that we require to God's unfailing love. Paul admonishes his readers to tap into the deep fountain of God's love in the same manner that the roots of a plant penetrate deep into the earth to find valuable sources of life-sustaining water.

Paul wants believers to do more than ponder God's love. He prescribed an intimate experience with Christ so that they would fully know His love. Paul's words speak prophetically to us today. He dares us to test the bounds of God's love. How wide is His love? How long? How high? How deep? When we experience God's love ourselves, we can only conclude as Paul did that it is unfathomable. More importantly, it never runs out.

God's Word came in the form of man that we might receive life in all its fullness (John 10:10). How did Christ secure that abundant life for us? He secured it by means of the greatest act of love known to mankind. He gave His life for you and me. This was not a one-time event. Even today He stands ready and willing to pour out His Spirit into our hearts if we will simply receive it. The Apostle John described God's essence as love (1 John 4:8). Therefore we are baptized with God's love when He baptizes us with His Spirit. This is the fullness of life and power that Paul described to the Ephesians. It is the power of God's love that fills our hearts and overflows in our soul. It is the fuel of life that never runs out as long as we stay connected to our source.

Love that Overflows

> *"Be imitators of God, therefore, as dearly loved children*
> *and live a life of love, just as Christ loved us and gave himself up for us*
> *as a fragrant offering and sacrifice to God." Ephesians 5:1-2, NIV*

Paul's words not only encourage us to draw strength from God's unfailing love but admonish us to share this Christ-like love with others. As children of God, we are expected to imitate Him in thought and deed, living a life filled with love for others. Christ demonstrated the extent of His love for us by offering His life in exchange for ours. If we desire to drink from the stream of God's love, we must allow it to flow through us and into the lives of others. This attitude of the heart ensures that our love tank will never be empty.

Paul's words bring to mind an anecdote in the Bible about a woman who desperately needed real love. Jesus was traveling to Judea and decided to pass through Samaria. This detail would be of little consequence except that the Jews and Samaritans did not associate with one another. The animosity between the two groups had persisted for many years despite their common heritage. Taking a break from the long journey, Jesus stopped to rest near a well in a small town of Samaria. During this break, He asked a woman who'd come to draw water for a drink.

The woman was surprised by Jesus' request for several reasons. First, it was uncommon and even inappropriate for a man in her culture to address a woman he did not know. Furthermore, she recognized that Jesus was a Jew and certainly did not expect a Jew to drink from the cup of a Samaritan. Jesus quickly moves the focus from natural things to spiritual matters, telling her about living water. Jesus promised that everyone who drinks from His living water would never thirst again. Moreover, He promised that His water would become an internal well leading to eternal life.

The woman now intrigued by Jesus' offer asks for some of His water. At this point the conversation becomes personal. Jesus instructs the woman to get her husband so that he might also partake. The woman does not realize who Jesus is or the deep insight He has into her life. The woman admits that she doesn't have a husband. Jesus, knowing this already, begins to tell her private things concerning her life. We come to find out that the woman had been married five times and was living with a man who was not her husband. Jesus continues to speak to her concerning her life and reveals His divine identity.

Everlasting Love

The account of the woman is quite amazing if you believe as I do that this was not a chance meeting. I believe that Jesus was in effect waiting for the woman to arrive. The woman was surely someone with a bad reputation. She had five husbands and lived with a man out of wedlock. This was not only a sinful lifestyle but would have made her a social outcast. One could reasonably conclude from her many failed relationships that the woman was desperately searching for love. Yet her self-esteem had been assaulted to such a degree that she'd relegated herself to a sinful physical relationship. Most people during her day, and even our day, would write her off as someone undeserving of true love.

Can you picture her arrival at the well that day? She had literally and figuratively run out of gas. A life devoid of real love is the antithesis of the abundant life that Jesus promises us. We must come to understand as this woman did that we need God's Spirit living on the inside. In order to successfully complete our journey in life, we must receive God's Spirit into our hearts. His Spirit, which Jesus described as living water, is the eternal fuel source that flows from within. When we allow His Spirit to live inside of us, His love (and our fuel source) is renewed every day.

The anecdote about the woman has a happy ending. She hurries to the town to tell others about Jesus. She in effect becomes His first witness in Samaria. We find that many of the people come to meet Jesus based on her testimony. Jesus stays and teaches the people for two days and many of them become believers of the gospel. The woman's story demonstrates that genuine love not only alters our course but propels us down the road of life. When we allow Christ to invade our hearts, we develop the capacity to genuinely love God, ourselves, and others. It is in this manner that we become imitators of God and guiding lights for others on the road of life.

Maybe you are like I was, or like the woman at the well, or like the countless others who have realized that their love tank is low or empty. The emptiness you feel takes away your motivation, courage, or energy to productively make your way down the road of life. I can personally attest that love is the answer. Moreover, there is nothing that compares to the love of God. The love of God is both unfailing and unconditional. God's love not only draws you closer to Him, but it strengthens your relationships with others. When you are loved by God, you are connected to your purpose in life and you have the power to pursue it wholeheartedly. Love for God and others compels us to be more than we could hope to be in our own strength. Love for God and others creates a constant flow of fuel, ensuring that our tank is never empty. As the Apostle Paul aptly put it, love never fails (1 Cor. 13:8).

●

Part
3

Stay
in Your
Lane

"You were running a good race.
Who cut in on you and kept you from obeying the truth?"
Galatians 5:7, NIV

Though tiny compared to its colossal competitors, the automotive company Subaru has endured as a relatively profitable company for decades. Subaru, which is the Japanese word for unite, was formed when five small Japanese automotive manufacturers merged after World War II. As global competition has intensified in the automotive sector, Subaru has built its reputation by focusing on the production of conventional passenger cars equipped with all-wheel-drive (AWD) systems. In fact in many markets, its entire product line has this feature.

All-wheel-drive systems improve traction when driving on wet pavement, snow, or ice. Though my grasp of automotive engineering is neither wide nor deep, I have a basic understanding of how all-wheel-drive technology works. The intelligent system actually selects the best manner to distribute power to the wheels based on driving conditions. For example, if a particular wheel is slipping, it directs power to the other wheels to improve traction. This functionality enables drivers to perform better during challenging driving conditions.

With this knowledge as a backdrop, I have a much greater appreciation for the advertising campaign that Subaru launched in February of 2006. The company signed American rock star Sheryl Crow and employed her hit tune from a decade earlier entitled "Every Day is a Winding Road." The tune makes perfect sense given Subaru's focus on passenger cars that adapt to difficult conditions. If the road is ever changing, and occasionally slippery, one might strongly consider parking a Subaru in the garage.

As I pondered the Subaru campaign, I was struck by how it also presented a metaphor for life. I often feel as though I am traveling down a winding road. Maybe you do as well. Along the road we encounter unexpected twists and turns. No matter where we find ourselves, we ultimately encounter inclement weather. As all experienced drivers know, inclement weather generally translates into difficult driving conditions. Success during life's journey is largely a function of our ability to navigate difficult terrain.

In a letter to the Galatians, the Apostle Paul admonishes them to stay on course. Paul had received reports that the fellowship was straying from the faith. They'd started confidently down the right path, but outside influences were causing them to veer off course. In a manner of speaking, they were losing traction. Have unexpected circumstances or outside influences ever caused you to veer off course in life? I've certainly made my share of wrong turns and even lost control at times. Through God's grace and guidance I've always managed to get back on track. Without His indwelling Spirit, I shudder to think where wrong turns might have taken me.

In writing to the Galatians, Paul uses the example of a Greek runner. In essence he compares the journey of life to a competitive race. The contestant in the race not only had to keep pace but also stay on course. Straying from the course would result in disqualification from the race. In life, we similarly must stay the course. The challenge is to prevent outside influences from hindering us. Paul pointedly asked his readers who was hindering them from obeying God's instructions. And while Paul acknowledges outside interference, Paul's focus is squarely on the contestant. It was the job of the contestant to stay on course and in turn the job of the hearer to obey the rules. Outside influences were akin to someone cutting in on a runner and impeding his or her progress.

In the great race of life, it is God who determines the course, sets the rules, and awards the prize. If we plan to safely reach our destination, we must stay in our lane. Said another way, we must observe the instructions that God gives us. God is a loving Father and cares for us dearly. As such, His commands are never onerous. The Bible testifies that His yoke is easy and His burden is light (Matt. 11:30). To ensure our success, God has given us His indwelling Spirit. The Spirit assists us during those inevitable times when we lose traction in order to make sure we stay in our lane. If we simply revere God and obey His Word, He will keep us on track.

•

⑨

Obey
the Rules
of the Road

"For what I do is not the good I want to do; no, the evil I do not want to do—
this I keep on doing. Now if I do what I do not want to do, it is no longer I who
do it, but it is sin living in me that does it. So I find this law at work:
When I want to do good, evil is right there with me. For in my inner being I
delight in God's law; but I see another law at work in the members of my
body, waging war against the law of my mind and making me a prisoner
of the law of sin at work within my members."
Romans 7:19-23, NIV

One day while searching for driving directions on the Internet, I began to consider the expansive network of roads, highways, and city streets that keep us all connected. We often take for granted the intricacy and thoughtfulness that goes into maintaining this ever evolving network. Later, as I drove toward my destination, my thoughts turned to the many signs and signals along the road. Everywhere I looked, there were different signs and signals. Some of the signs provided direction while others helped me chart my progress. Certain signs informed me of changing road conditions or traffic patterns. There were signs that informed me of the appropriate speed to travel while certain signals instructed me as to when I should stop or proceed. The signs and signals perfectly complement the intricate road system. As long as I carefully observe the signs and signals along the way, they enable me to safely arrive at my predetermined destination.

As a believer in Christ, I've come to realize that life is largely about the journey. Early on in the text we established that every journey must begin and end with the destination. The destination first is seen in the mind's eye and subsequently becomes a reality through a purposeful search. If we accept that eternal life with Christ is our ultimate destination, then the exercise boils down to determining the route that will take us there. While life is challenging at times, it is not the mystery that many would have us believe. God, through His Spirit, provides clear direction to those who choose to follow Him. The qualification being that we must actively seek His instruction. In essence, we must have our spiritual eyes open and we must faithfully observe the signs and signals He gives us.

As I consider my own life, my challenges have usually come in the area of faith. There have been many instances when I believe that God has spoken to me or shown me things with respect to the direction He wants me to take. The question generally boils down to whether I lean to my own understanding or determine what it is that God would have me to do. I believe we all have a similar challenge as we travel down life's winding road. With so many distractions and competing influences, our judgment can become impaired. At times we miss the signals God sends us, or, worse, we ignore them outright. If life is largely about the journey, then the wise traveler must discipline him or herself to obey the rules of the road.

Road Rules

In his letter to the believers in Rome, the Apostle Paul captures the essence of the internal struggle we all face as we make our way down the road of life. Paul observed that though he approached each day with the best intentions, he often made inappropriate choices. Paul concluded that the challenge was less of an intellectual one and more of a spiritual one. In fact, Paul readily admitted that he was knowledgeable of God's laws or instructions. Paul identified the culprit as an internal one, attacking the subconscious level of the heart. Paul goes as far as describing the internal struggle as a war in his mind.

Have you ever felt like Paul? I'll bet you have. I know that I have. I believe the vast majority of people start each day with the best intentions. Moreover, the individual who believes in God certainly wants to do God's will. However, being in the driver's seat can bring out the best and the worst in us as we travel down the road of life. For example, how many of you have ever run a red light? Have you ever consciously driven above the speed limit? Have you ever run a stop sign? What about cutting off another driver because you didn't check your blind spot or, worse, you were talking on your cell phone? Have you ever gotten lost because you were too proud or too preoccupied to ask for directions? Any one of these infractions would not qualify us as the best or the safest driver. Yet I suspect many of us have made them all over the course of our lives.

What do driving infractions have to do with everyday life? They are a strong metaphor for our spiritual lives. If we are honest, most of these infractions are avoidable. Though we are reticent to admit it, the infractions that I mentioned (and countless others I didn't) occur because we make a conscious choice to disregard the rules of the road. This may seem inconsequential save the fact that those rules work together for a very important purpose. The rules and the accompanying signs and signals we encounter on the road of life are there to ensure that we safely arrive at our appointed destination. When we overlook or ignore the rules of the road, we endanger our lives as well as the lives of others.

The Apostle Paul deftly dealt with the issue of obedience in his letter to believers in Rome. Paul describes individuals who willfully disobey God's instructions as carnally minded. Paul's implication is that this type of individual is motivated by selfish desires. Left to our own devices, our motives and actions are often contrary to the will of God. This mindset leads to poor decisions and disastrous results. Paul encourages us to faithfully seek and abide by God's instructions. This type of individual displays true wisdom and is described by Paul as spiritually minded (Rom. 8:6). This type of mindset results in a prosperous life and a successful life journey.

Being spiritually minded simply means that as I travel down the road of life I will consciously seek God's will as opposed to my own. It also means that when I receive God's instructions I will obey, even if it seems uncomfortable or inconvenient from my perspective. The spiritually minded individual understands that God's instructions are not arbitrary but rather are given with our best interest in mind. The spiritually minded individual also understands that God's indwelling Spirit is necessary to perceive and interpret the signs and signals we encounter as we navigate the challenging road of life.

The Driver's Seat

"So, dear brothers and sisters, you have no obligation whatsoever to do what your sinful nature urges you to do. For if you keep on following it you will perish. But if through the power of the Holy Spirit you turn from it and its evil deeds, you will live. For all who are led by the Spirit of God are children of God."
Romans 8:12-14, NLT

Anyone who has sat in the passenger seat of my automobile would attest that I am a fairly conservative driver. While I've certainly violated a road rule or two during the course of my driving days, I tend to stay on the straight and narrow path. In fact, I haven't been cited for a traffic violation since my first year as a driver. Though it's been quite a long time since my last citation, I can still remember the incident as if it were yesterday.

I'd held down a job during much of my high school career, and my father rewarded me by helping me purchase an automobile. I was the first among my neighborhood friends to own a car, which of course earned me the coveted role of designated driver. One evening my friends dropped by my house and invited me to the mall. Of course this was their way if asking for a lift. Although I wasn't particularly interested in going to the mall, they successfully convinced me to go.

After an uneventful evening we piled into my car and headed for home. I'm probably stating the obvious when I tell you that if five teenagers are in an automobile, the driver may get distracted from time to time. Unfortunately for me, this was one of those times. A changing traffic signal caught me off guard and I made a bad decision to accelerate through the intersection. It didn't help that my backseat drivers encouraged me to do so. As fate would have it, a police car was at the intersection waiting for the light to change. I didn't make it a block before the police lights were flashing behind me. This certainly wasn't the way that I'd hoped to end my evening.

After a short lecture the police officer took my license in exchange for a fifty-five-dollar ticket. That may not sound like much in today's dollars, but it was a significant sum for a high school student with a part-time job. Moreover, I was concerned about the way my parents would react. I hadn't been reckless in my driving or decision making. However, my lack of attentiveness did result in a careless decision. The rest of the ride home was pretty quiet so I was left to ponder my actions.

First, I questioned why I'd ventured to the mall in the first place. Initially there was a bit of resentment toward my friends. After all, they dragged me off to the mall against my wishes. My initial reaction was characteristic of how we often react when our decisions result in adverse consequences. It must be someone else's fault. Part of being responsible means that we readily accept the due consequences of our decisions. Whether I was persuaded or otherwise, I was the individual sitting in the driver's seat. Regardless of the many influences we encounter in life, we ultimately must make our own decisions.

Next, I began to think how unfortunate my timing was. Why did the police officer have to be waiting at that particular intersection? Why didn't we leave a few minutes earlier? Why didn't we leave a few minutes later? Another common response is to chalk adverse outcomes up to luck or fate. It's much easier for us to accept that we were victims of bad luck or that the situation was beyond our control. This absolves us from the need to critically examine our motives or decision making. However, the Bible affirms that while God is actively involved in our lives we are the ultimate masters of our fate. Everything we do in this life has sure consequences.

Next my thoughts turned toward the reprisal of my actions. I wasn't looking forward to the not-so-modest bite that the city of Chicago would be taking out of my next paycheck. If I wanted to keep my driving record intact, I would have to sit through a half-day safe driving course. This of course would involve a fifteen-dollar surcharge, bringing the total cost of my infraction to seventy dollars. These thoughts catapulted me into the woe-is-me syndrome. As we mature in life, we learn that remorse is not the same as repentance. At that point I was simply concerned about myself and was neither accountable nor repentant for my actions. The repentant heart not only acknowledges the error of one's ways but is committed to choosing a different course in the future.

As I pulled up to my house I was already dreading the conversation with my father. To my surprise, he wasn't angry. Instead he was disappointed, which actually felt worse. My father reminded me that owning an automobile was a privilege that came with significant responsibility. Each time I got into the driver's seat I was accountable to myself, my passengers, and other drivers. My decisions behind the wheel could have life or death consequences. As such, he expected me to obey the rules of the road so that everyone impacted by my actions would arrive at their destinations safely. I never forgot that conversation with my father. I'd like to believe it made me a better driver and a better person.

Backseat Driver

Most people have little tolerance for the dreaded *backseat* driver. You know the type of person that I am referring to. They always seem to know a better or faster way to get where you are going. They never quite like your style of driving. It's either too fast or too slow. It's too aggressive or too cautious. What's more they tend not to like the backseat and prefer to cozy up right next to you in the front passenger seat. Maybe some of you are best friends with this type of person. Maybe some of you are married to this type of person. Whatever the case, there is generally a battle of wills once a driver gets behind the wheel.

Drivers by their nature don't like to be told how to drive. This interesting attribute of the human construct makes the Apostle Paul's advice to the believers at Rome all the more intriguing. Paul tells his readers that we don't have to succumb to our own selfish nature. Though our intentions are good, our nature is often at odds with that of our Creator. To bring our will in line with His, He offers to dwell with us. All we have to do is invite Him in. This is exactly what Paul suggests. Paul lets us know that it is only through the power of God's Spirit that we can safely complete life's journey. He preaches the virtue of enlisting the service of the ultimate *Backseat* Driver.

Recall from chapter 1 that we made a clear distinction between passengers and drivers on the road of life. The driver seeks to master his or her own destiny, which is a proactive disposition. This is not a character flaw, rather a God-given trait. We are created in God's image and have a mandate to establish dominion in the earth. We can not reasonably expect to manage the things of God without first learning to manage our own circumstances. We established that proficiency behind the wheel of an automobile comes through careful observance of the rules of the road. Similarly, success in life results from careful obedience to God's Word.

Mastery of our destiny is not only desirable but it is readily attainable. Yet the Apostle Paul correctly warns us that leaning to our own understanding jeopardizes our journey. In fact, doing so ultimately leads to one's demise. It is the individual that humbles him or herself and accepts the leading of God's Spirit that finds true happiness and success in this world and the kingdom to come. The Holy Spirit is our gift from God to accompany us on the road of life. Since our safe travel depends on observance of the rules of the road, the Holy Spirit acts as both our guide and an interpreter along the way.

•

Drive Defensively

"If you have any encouragement from being united with Christ,
if any comfort from his love, if any fellowship with the Spirit,
if any tenderness and compassion, then make my joy complete by
being like-minded, having the same love, being one in spirit and purpose.
Do nothing out of selfish ambition or vain conceit,
but in humility consider others better than yourselves."
Philippians 2:1-3, NIV

The National Safety Council reports that each year in the United States there are over 41,000 fatalities and over 2 million disabling injuries as a result of motor vehicle accidents. While these statistics are disconcerting, the more troubling reality is that the vast majority of these fatalities and injuries are preventable. If motorists simply employed the defensive driving tactics that are routinely taught in driver's education courses across the nation, the statistics could be markedly reduced.

With the threat of difficult driving conditions, unexpected hazards, and impaired or inattentive motorists, driving demands our full attention. Regardless of a driver's experience or skill, even a momentary lapse can lead to dire consequences. Moreover, driving defensively is not only about taking responsibility for our individual actions. A responsible driver is also mindful of the actions of other drivers. As driving goes, we are indeed the keepers of our brothers and sisters.

As we travel down the road of life, the same defensive driving principles apply. While each of us embarks on a unique journey, we have a common destiny. This common destiny means that our lives are intertwined with the lives of others. As we travel toward our divinely appointed destination, we are accountable for ourselves as well as the other individuals whom our lives touch. Driving defensively means that we are sensitive to the leading of God's Spirit, and we are sensitive to the impact that our actions have on others.

The Apostle Paul's letter to the Philippians provides insight regarding our responsibility to our fellow drivers on the road of life. Philippi was a culturally diverse Roman City and in turn the church at Philippi reflected this diversity. The Bible specifically mentions Roman, Greek, and Asian members and there were undoubtedly other ethnicities represented. The church also was diverse with respect to social status. It would not have been uncommon for a slave and a wealthy business owner to worship alongside one another. Paul undoubtedly taught the Philippians that there was no distinction between classes or ethnicities in the body of Christ.

Paul had a special place in his heart for the Philippians. In a world separated by ethnic and class distinctions, the believers at Philippi demonstrated the love of Christ in their daily interactions with one another. It is important to note that this behavior was a result of sound instruction and the influence of the Holy Spirit. Paul taught the fellowship that though they each faced an individual course, their mutual love and support for one another would aid them in their individual journeys. Paul further challenged them to be self-less in their dealings, admonishing them to put the interests of others ahead of their own. In essence, Paul advocated the virtues of defensive driving. Their responsibility was not simply to mind their own affairs. Paul encouraged them to work toward the mutual benefit of the broader community of believers.

In an era when people have become decidedly more individualistic in their attitudes, the truth of Paul's inspired words should speak clearly to our hearts. Paul's message to us is clear. We must begin to see life's journey from God's perspective. Our journey is not independent from our fellow travelers, but interdependent. Those who rely on the wisdom of God have come to understand that interdependence is actually the highest form of maturity. As we grow spiritually, we realize that the expression of true humility is the characteristic that makes us most like Christ. It is when we respect and serve the needs of others that we discover the unique manner in which God uses our individual talents. When we help to ensure the safe travel of others, we demonstrate the attitude of Christ.

What Would Jesus Teach?

"Each of you should look not only to your own interests, but also to the interests of others. Your attitude should be the same as that of Christ Jesus: Who, being in very nature God, did not consider equality with God something to be grasped, but made himself nothing, taking the very nature of a servant, being made in human likeness." Philippians 2:4-7, NIV

Surely you've seen or heard the phrase. Maybe you've seen it on a bumper sticker or a T-shirt. Maybe you've heard it as a byline in a Sunday sermon or as a gentle reminder from a good friend. *What would Jesus do?* It's a provocative question regardless of your religious affiliation. Why, you might ask? Well as reputations go, Jesus of Nazareth aka Jesus the Christ has arguably the most notable rep in history. As such, the question invokes a response from people of all walks of life. Jesus is acknowledged by friend and foe for his incredible compassion. This implies that Jesus' response to a given situation would almost certainly be uncommon by most people's standards.

However, this is the standard that Paul puts forth in his letter to the Philippians. He challenges his readers to move beyond their own motivations and instead respond with an attitude resembling that of Christ Jesus.

As I pondered my concept of driving under the influence, it begged a related question. *How would Jesus drive?* As I considered Paul's depiction of Christ, I noticed time and again that he highlighted Jesus' humility. Despite sharing the very nature of God, He took on the form of fallen man. Moreover, He sacrificed His will and even His life for the well-being of His fellow travelers on the road of life. If defensive driving is largely about being respectful and considerate of others, I suspect Jesus would be as defensive a driver as you could find. He certainly wouldn't disregard the rules of the road or violate the speed limit. I suspect He'd have no problem yielding the right of way and He'd always signal His intentions. He invented the term *Good Samaritan* so He'd undoubtedly stop to help stranded motorists or go out of His way to give others a lift.

The more I thought about it, I realized the wisdom in Paul's writing. Paul challenged his readers by holding up the ultimate standard. Paul was quite the role model himself, having dedicated his own life to the cause of Christ. However, Paul does not suggest that we imitate his attitude. Instead he sets the loftiest of goals. He encourages us all to adopt the mind of Christ. As we make our way down the road of life, we have a simple yet full-proof litmus test. When we encounter important decisions, particularly as it relates to our interactions with other people, we should ask ourselves one question. *What would Jesus do?* When we learn to humble ourselves and submit to the leading of God's Spirit as Jesus did, we set a wonderful example for others.

Now that we've considered the matter of how Jesus would drive, it is only natural to consider the corollary question. *What would Jesus teach?* Specifically, what defensive driving principles would Jesus teach? After all, Jesus was a world-renowned teacher with numerous students and followers. Jesus also had an incredible knack for distilling biblical truths from everyday experiences. It's not a stretch to surmise that if Jesus had been born in the present day that He might have used parables pertaining to driving to teach His students. With this in mind I will offer seven principles that Jesus might teach as it relates to defensive driving on the road of life.

Defensive Driving Principle #1: Be Courteous

In an overcaffeinated society, patience simply isn't the virtue it once was. If you don't believe me, simply observe your fellow drivers the next time you are caught in rush-hour traffic. It is puzzling to witness the battles that are fought over small pieces of real estate. People often avoid signaling their intentions to change lanes for fear that their fellow drivers will speed up to claim previously unoccupied pavement. Somehow it no longer matters that signaling a lane change is one of the most basic disciplines taught in drivers' education. When in doubt about who has the right of way, a defensive driver abides by a simple credo. Yield! This simple act of humility will help to ensure the safe travel of many. After all, courtesy is often contagious.

Jesus spent a lot of time instructing His disciples about this principle. In fact, He considered it one of the single most important things that He taught. He told his disciples that the greatest commandment of all is to love God and by extension obey His commandments. We discussed observance of God's commands in the previous chapter. A close second in Jesus' book is to love our neighbors as we love ourselves (Mark 12:30-31). If we manage to get this right, the rest of the principles come naturally. How would you treat yourself if you were in the other car? Would you yield? Would you signal? Would you slow down? Just in case we get hung up on semantics, Jesus also instructed his students to love their enemies and those who might mistreat them (Luke 6:27). As best as I can tell, His call for courteousness covers everyone on the road.

Defensive Driving Principle #2: Pay Attention

Whether daydreaming, distracted, fatigued, or impaired, drivers cite inattentiveness as the root cause of most accidents. I would also venture to guess that some form of inattentiveness was the root cause of virtually all of your driving miscues. Think of all the driving mistakes you've made over the years. Even if you are a conscientious driver (and I hope you are), I suspect this list is longer than you care to admit. Your personal experience alone should underscore the need to pay attention when you get behind the wheel of a motor vehicle. Like it or not, people invariably make driving mistakes.

The defensive driver not only guards against his or her inattentiveness but makes allowances for the mistakes of other drivers.

Jesus said it best when He instructed His disciples to watch and pray (Mark 14:38). This was not just a one-time admonishment but a daily frame of mind. In no uncertain terms, He instructed them to stay alert and to stay connected to God. Jesus knew that temptation awaited the disciples at every turn. This is similarly true for us as we travel down the road of life. While our inner man is willing to submit to God, our selfish desires can get in the way if we don't pay attention. Spiritual attentiveness assures that we are mindful of the signs and signals that God sends our way. Spiritual attentiveness also means that we use discernment with respect to the actions of others. Constant prayer helps us discern God's will concerning our lives and others we touch.

Defensive Driving Principle #3: Slow Down

Excessive speed is often a factor in fatal collisions. Every increment of speed above the recommended speed limit reduces your ability to react to hazardous conditions or the unexpected actions of other motorists. While excessive speed risks lives, it generally saves little or no time. Surely you've zipped by a fellow motorist only to have them pull up beside you at the next traffic light or at the next freeway exit. Speeding generally wastes fuel, wears down your brakes, and increases your stress level. So the next time you are having a bout of anxiety and you feel like life is speeding out of control, I offer two words of advice. Slow down!

Jesus gives some very sound advice to His disciples who are anxious over a great many things. He tells them not to worry about tomorrow, because tomorrow will bring its own challenges (Matt. 6:34). This directive came in the midst of a teaching concerning faith. Jesus was implying that much of our anxiety is a function of our lack of faith. We become harried emotionally and physically as we dart from activity to activity chasing an elusive sense of contentment. The key is to realize that the contentment we desperately seek can only be found when we are in the will of God. This is why we must slow down so that we hear what the Spirit is speaking to our hearts.

Defensive Driving Principle #4: Be Sober

A clear no-no for anyone getting behind the wheel of a motor vehicle is driving while impaired. Impairment means that there is an influence that decreases your ability to operate your vehicle safely. As driving goes, alcohol is a prime cause of impairment. Alcohol is a depressant that greatly reduces one's attentiveness and decision-making ability. Prescription and non-prescription drugs are agents that also can impair one's driving ability. Driving requires you to have your full wits about you. Driving a motor vehicle requires mental awareness. Likewise, driving down the road of life requires us to be spiritually aware.

Jesus' admonishment for sobriety is best reflected in the words of one of his prized pupils. In a letter to like-minded believers, the Apostle Peter encouraged them on three separate occasions to be sober, or exercise self-control (1 Pet. 1:3). They should be wary of any outside influence that might compromise disciplined decision making. Peter undoubtedly received his instruction directly from Jesus. As we go through life, there is a constant battle to influence our decisions. It is our responsibility to reject any outside influence that would compromise our willingness or ability to submit to the leading of God's Spirit.

Defensive Driving Principle #5: Restrain Yourself

As much as we wish that it weren't the case, accidents do happen. While attentiveness and courteousness can help us avoid many accidents altogether, there are still precautions we can and should take in case the unexpected occurs. The first and best line of defense against severe or fatal injury in a car accident is the use of a seat belt. Pure and simple, seat belts save lives. Despite laws that mandate the use of safety belts, an alarming number of individuals ignore this important precaution. It is also interesting to note that males sixteen to twenty-five, statistically the highest-risk drivers, are the least likely to buckle up. This underscores an interesting human trait. Immature individuals often reject restraint.

One of the surest signs of maturity is the application of self-restraint. As we established early in the text, free choice doesn't mean free reign. Jesus teaches plainly that if we love Him we will keep His commandments (John 14:15). Notice that the decision is ultimately mine and yours. We demonstrate our maturity by restraining ourselves. Our faith in the Word of God is what protects us on the road of life. On one occasion the Apostle Paul describes faith as a shield (Eph. 6:16). The Holy Spirit reminds us of God's instructions in our time of need. So while chance and circumstance befall us all on the road of life, the driver who is restrained through faith in God can endure any of life's trials.

Defensive Driving Principle #6: Calm Down

When your emotions are running high, the first thing to fail is usually your judgment. A great many mistakes happen when people are angry or upset. You cannot afford to drive when you are emotionally distressed. Let me repeat that statement. You cannot afford to drive when you are emotionally distressed! In the same manner that you put your physical life in danger when driving under duress, you put your spiritual well-being in danger when you make decisions under emotional duress. The answer in both circumstances is the same. Calm down! Do not proceed and do not pass go until you are emotionally stable and the Holy Spirit is leading you.

Jesus frequently taught His disciples of the importance of their emotional stability. His desire for them was that they would have peace. Peace is a state of emotional security and tranquility. To be clear, peace does not imply the absence of conflict or tribulation. Peace speaks to one's inward condition regardless of the external conditions. Jesus taught the disciples that in this world they would encounter tribulation. His teachings were about how they should respond to the inevitable challenges that they would face on the road of life. It was by conquering Himself and His emotions that Jesus overcame the cares of the world and successfully completed His journey. Through His Spirit, Jesus offers us the same peace (John 16:33).

Defensive Driving Principle #7: Lose the Ego

Tell me if this scenario sounds familiar. You're traveling down the freeway carefully observing the speed limit. Okay, so maybe you are a tad over the speed limit. At any rate, you notice in your rearview mirror a vehicle barreling down the road behind you. Before you know it, the vehicle is riding so close you can see the expression on the driver's face in your rearview mirror. So much for all that talk about being considerate. This driver wants you out of the way and he or she has decided to enforce their will upon you. You wonder to yourself if the driver ever learned the rule that advises to maintain a following distance of at least two car lengths. Does this scenario sound familiar? Maybe the situation is worse and you were the perpetrator in the rearview mirror. Drivers need space so we would all be best served if we lose the ego. We don't have the road all to ourselves so we shouldn't drive as though we do.

Jesus teaches a simple yet powerful lesson in regard to this principle. Jesus tells us simply that blessed are the meek because they will inherit the earth (Matt. 5:5). The term *meek* should not be confused with the term *weak*. Meek refers to having a gentle spirit. Only a person with some degree of power can truly display the quality of meekness. When we are traveling down the road of life, we may at times have the desire to impose our will on others. However, this attitude is the opposite of Christ's example and will not be rewarded by God. The individual brave enough to tackle the open road yet respectful enough to share it with others will ultimately be successful in life. Driving defensively requires that we adopt the mindset of Christ, placing the welfare of others before that of our own. Humility goes a long way in life. In fact, humility paves the road to eternity if we simply choose to follow it.

•

Expect Delays

"God is not unjust; he will not forget your work and the love you have shown
him as you have helped his people and continue to help them.
We want each of you to show this same diligence to the very end, in order to
make your hope sure. We do not want you to become lazy, but to imitate those
who through faith and patience inherit what has been promised."
Hebrews 6:10-12, NIV

Picture the following scene. You are one of countless motorists the world over braving rush-hour traffic as you make your way to work or school. Although traffic is heavy, it's moving briskly. This is comforting given the fact that you departed ten minutes later than usual this morning. As you make your way around a bend on the freeway you notice a sea of red lights ahead. As you pump the brakes to bring the car to a stop, you can feel your blood pressure rising. Although traffic delays are a regular part of the weekly commute, it's difficult to get accustomed to them. Maybe the delay wouldn't be as irksome if you weren't behind schedule. Who are we kidding? Even if you'd departed according to your regular schedule you'd have struggled to arrive at the proper time and with the proper attitude.

When freeways are packed to the max, as they generally are during rush hour, it doesn't take much to bring traffic to a grinding halt. This is a very inconvenient truth for hundreds of millions of motorists the world over. After all, freeways are intended to speed things along. Nevertheless, a delay impacting countless motorists can be caused by a single incident. While the incident could be a major accident, most delays result from minor events that happen with regularity.

Let's continue with the scene from before. There you are, sitting in a virtual parking lot. If you're like me, you're straining your neck to peer down the road. You desperately want to know the cause of the delay. More importantly, you'd like to get an idea of how long it will be before traffic picks up again. Although you have no knowledge of the actual cause of the delay, you're convinced it's the result of poor driving. Why can't everyone else drive as carefully as you? Isn't it interesting how sanctimonious we become when evaluating the driving ability of others?

So what caused the traffic jam anyway? If we travel several miles up the road and rewind the tape, we find our friend John Driver heading to the office. John is zipping along when a large piece of debris falls from a pickup truck in front of him. As John veers out of his lane, Mary Motorist is cut off and quickly taps her brakes to avoid hitting John. Joe Trucker is behind Mary Motorist driving an eighteen wheeler with a huge payload. By the time Joe notices Mary decelerating, he has little time to react. Joe stomps on his brakes and veers to avoid Mary. With each link in the chain, the reaction times become shorter. A chorus line of cars eventually has to slam on the brakes. With so many cars on the freeway, a traffic jam quickly occurs.

The reverberations from an incident like the one described can easily stretch for miles. Although an actual collision was averted, it takes several minutes for traffic to get going again. Moreover, any number of seemingly innocuous events can trigger a traffic jam. With this knowledge in mind, it is no wonder that traffic delays are a rule and not an exception. Again, delays are a rule and not an exception! As travelers on the road of life, our biggest challenge is often our perspective. If delays are indeed an inevitable part of life, we must learn to expect delays and keep our emotions and subsequent actions in check.

The writer of the epistle to the Hebrews gets to the heart of the issue as it regards delays on the road of life. This too is closely linked to our faith. The writer, believed by many to be the Apostle Paul, reminds us that God is not unjust. Though circumstances may seem to suggest otherwise, God's scales of justice are always perfectly balanced. He both sees and weighs our actions. Moreover, He weighs our actions in the broader context of His sovereign plan. God has a just reward in store for each of us based on our faithfulness. In order for us to receive the things that God has in store for us and reach our ultimate destination, we must be prepared to handle life's inevitable delays.

Fair-weather Friend

"Do not throw away this confident trust in the Lord,
no matter what happens. Remember the great reward it brings you!
Patient endurance is what you need now, so you will continue to do God's will.
Then you will receive all that he has promised."
Hebrews 10:35-36, NLT

Let's face it. Most of us have been conditioned to expect immediate gratification. As such, we often struggle when things don't happen when and how we desire. Whether you are starting a family or starting a business, I offer a practical piece of advice. Expect delays! God's Word affirms that we will encounter unexpected events and circumstances. We often become disheartened because we do not maintain the proper perspective. We must remain emotionally stable and spiritually grounded so that we make faith-based decisions. It is through faith and patience that we receive the promises that God has reserved for us.

The writer of the epistle to the Hebrews challenges us to do something that is not only difficult but foreign to the average individual. The writer suggests plainly and concretely that we place our full confidence in God no matter what occurs. In fact, his admonishment implies that many people jettison their faith in God when delays or challenges arise. Why might this be the case you ask? I believe it occurs as a result of a lack of true fellowship. The majority of people in the world are monotheists, accepting that there is one God. Despite strong cultural traditions and religious activities that support this viewpoint, few people expect or experience the personal relationship with God that is depicted by the examples in the Bible.

Religion without fellowship can never engender true faith. There simply is no practical basis to develop the confident trust that the writer espouses. This also applies to situations where fellowship is not maintained and the relationship is severed. If we don't allow God's Spirit to live on the inside of us, we are left to interpret life's events from our own limited perspective. When delays come, and they will come, we feel as though we have failed or, worse, that God has failed us. So what do we do? We lose patience. We lose patience with our circumstances, the people around us, and ultimately with God. We must trust that God has our best interest in mind. God is not a fair-weather friend. By contrast, He is a friend who sticks closer than a brother.

Patiently Waiting

Inasmuch as honesty is the best policy and the bedrock of good communication, let me break the ice. Patience has not historically been my strong suit. While I can attest that through God's grace I have improved in this area, it is still an aspect of my character that requires attention. In defense of my psyche, I believe my aversion to waiting is related to the unique way that God has fashioned my temperament. Nonetheless, the ability to exercise patience is a very desirable character trait. As we established earlier, character is largely a function of choice.

Some of my most enduring lessons in life have come from interactions with my children. Through my children, God has instilled in me a greater appreciation for responsibility, stewardship, sacrifice, and unconditional love to highlight just a few areas. However, if I were asked to articulate a single virtue my children have demanded most of me it is the ability to exercise patience. To be clear, I have absolutely wonderful children. I thank God every day that they have so many of their mother's wonderful qualities. Yet as anyone with children will attest, they teach you an awful lot about yourself.

In my case they have often reminded me of the vital necessity to exercise patience.

Mealtime is an important time for family bonding. Even though our children are young, my wife and I cherish the time that we spend sharing our meals. Given my limited culinary skills, my wife bears the brunt of the cooking duties. As such, I believe the least that the boys and I can do is to dutifully clean our plates. While my boys have the best of intentions, this is where our differing perspectives and maturity come into play. My experiences with my sons are quite different given their unique personalities.

My older son, Javon, demonstrates some of the stereotypical qualities of a first child. He is very conscientious, extroverted, and sensitive to the opinions of others. His orientation at mealtime is very much social. While he appreciates his favorite foods, he is the pickiest eater of the bunch. Eating often takes a backseat to the social interaction. Left to his own devices he will chat and play until everyone else has finished. This often keeps me at the dinner table longer than I intend and tests the bounds of my patience.

My younger son, Micah, is much more reserved than his brother. This should not to be confused with being shy, which people quickly realize once they spend time with him. He simply socializes on his own terms. Micah is very independent. He is equally comfortable playing with a group of pre-schoolers or playing by himself in his room. He prefers to tackle most tasks without assistance. His persona is strikingly similar to my wife's. As such, he shares her even temperament, ingenuity, and tough-mindedness.

Micah's orientation at mealtime is fairly utilitarian. By that I mean that it's not difficult to get him to focus on the matter at hand. Most days he will finish his meal with little prompting as his brother entertains his tablemates. However, the operative word is *most*. There are occasions, some more memorable than others, when he is not in the best mood. As you might have guessed, his mood is directly correlated with his appetite. Good mood, good appetite and vice versa. When his iron will kicks in, daddy's patience wears thin.

A Little More Patience

My experiences at the dinner table mirror experiences in life. During our first family sit-down dinners I was quite regimented. I'd typically arrive from a busy day at work eager to get through the meal and on to other tasks. There were clothes to sort, mail to read, and bills to pay. Isn't it interesting to note how we project our attitude on others? I was in a hurry so it naturally felt like the boys were moving in slow motion. I'd ask, "Why does it take so long to finish your string beans?"

We often expect others to adjust to our pace without being sensitive to their needs. My oldest son has helped his father learn a good deal in this respect. Javon will see me off in the morning when everyone else is fast asleep. He is always eager to talk to me when I return home. Inasmuch as I often arrive just as dinner is being served, I've learned that I have to exercise patience to ensure that I am properly meeting my family's emotional needs. As I have become more responsive to Javon's desire to socialize at dinner, I've made an interesting discovery. The entire family has a more enjoyable experience at the dinner table... even if it takes us a little longer.

Micah has taught me a different aspect of patience. When he has his moments, I've come to learn that they're just that. Moments! It is true that in a battle of wills the parent will prevail more than not. However, these are generally hollow victories. I've learned that it is often wiser to exercise patience and allow my son to decide for himself. This does not mean that we forgo discipline when appropriate. However, the key is to apply discipline when it's appropriate as opposed to when I have lost patience. As I've learned to be more patient, I've developed greater insight into Micah's personality. He is both ingenious and tenacious. These traits will serve him well in whatever assignments God has in store for him. With patience I can better nurture my sons so that they can develop into strong godly men.

The lessons that I've learned at the dinner table are the same lessons that we all must learn in life. The first lesson involves pace. As we stated earlier in the text, the Bible warns us to be anxious for nothing. We are often in such a hurry to move on to the next task or achievement that we do not enjoy our lives in the manner that God intends. One of the most gratifying experiences of my day is dinnertime with my family. So why should I let the cares of this world cause me to rush through it? What about you? Do you find yourself racing from one thing to the next? Is keeping up with the Joneses running you down and stealing your joy? I've got a suggestion for you. Run your own race and move at the pace that God sets for you. In this way you will fully enjoy your relationship with God and others.

The second lesson involves endurance. I've often marveled that many people's greatest desire is something that God never promises – a life of total comfort. In fact, God not only assures us that we will encounter challenges in life but tells us that these challenges are intended to build our character and prepare us for future opportunities. Unfortunately, far too many people opt out before the benefit comes. My simple definition for patience is the proper investment of time. We naturally desire the benefits derived from a productive life. However, we must be willing to invest the proper amount of time. Are you in a hurry to get a new job, get a new house, or get a new spouse? Chances are that you are like the rest of us and you simply need more patience.

Patience was a virtue that the Apostle Paul regularly espoused. One can only surmise that this virtue was instilled in him through his incredible life journey. Paul may have best captured the relationship between God's Word and the human experience in a letter to believers in Rome. Paul concluded that the written record of God's Word is intended to give us hope as we patiently wait on God's promises (Rom. 15:4). Paul assures us that hope in God never fails. As you encounter life's ups and downs you must steady yourself on a foundation that is sure. Place your confidence in God's Word and let your daily prayer be a little more patience. Patience is the key that will unlock many doors during your journey in life.

●

Chapter

12

Ask
for
Assistance

"That is why we have a great High Priest who has gone to heaven,
Jesus the Son of God. Let us cling to him and never stop trusting him.
This High Priest of ours understands our weaknesses,
for he faced all of the same temptations we do, yet he did not sin.
So let us come boldly to the throne of our gracious God. There we will receive
his mercy, and we will find grace to help us when we need it."
Hebrews 4:14-16, NLT

The scene was the annual Thanksgiving dinner in 1997. My wife and I were visiting with family and enjoying the regular holiday traditions. One such tradition was the Thanksgiving Day football game that is televised each year. Every true American football fan knows that the Detroit Lions and Dallas Cowboys each host annual pigskin classics. Family, food, and football are the things that I've associated with Thanksgiving as long as I can remember. That year was especially memorable because the Lions were playing our beloved Chicago Bears. Though my wife is not a Chicago native, she is an avid football fan. Now family, food, and football are a shared Thanksgiving tradition that we are passing down to our children.

General Motors, then the largest automobile manufacturer in the world, chose the Lions-Bears telecast to air its first television commercial for its revolutionary OnStar system. For those who are unfamiliar with it, OnStar is a safety system that keeps motorists connected to a source of information and assistance while on the road. OnStar utilizes Global Positioning System (GPS) satellite technology to link the vehicle to an OnStar Center. At the touch of a button, an expertly trained advisor is available to offer real-time assistance twenty-four hours a day, 365 days a year. The system is voice activated, allowing hands-free access. In the event of a moderate or severe crash, the system will automatically send a message to the OnStar Center on the motorist's behalf.

From the time the OnStar system was introduced at the 1996 auto show, there was quite a buzz in the marketplace. At the time, it sounded like something out of a Star Trek movie. The football game was widely televised and was a good venue for the inaugural airing of the TV ad. In the commercial, a family is traveling on a dark stormy night. They are in a remote location making their way down an unfamiliar road. As if their situation wasn't difficult enough, the fuel indicator light flashes, informing the driver that he is low on fuel. His young son, who has been nervously observing in the back seat, begins to visualize dangerous scenarios such as the family stranded on the side of the road. Just as the boy's imagination begins to run wild, his father contacts OnStar. The helpful advisor directs the family to a service station a short distance away, underscoring the virtues of the innovative safety system.

The Thanksgiving Day premiere was the first installment of a highly effective television campaign. The third installment depicted the popular superhero Batman making use of the technology in his vaunted Batmobile. While we know Batman is a mythical character, the kid in all of us says if it's good enough for the caped crusader, it's good enough for me. Moreover, the advertisements drove home a simple concept. Driving circumstances are unpredictable and potential hazards wait around every corner. When traveling down the open road, it's safer to be connected to a knowledgeable source that watches over us at all times. The OnStar system is so highly valued that GM has made it an option for most of its modern fleet.

Wouldn't it be great to have the same type of safety as you travel on the road of life? Could you benefit from access to an expert advisor twenty-four hours a day, seven days a week? What if your advisor stood ready to intervene in your circumstances whenever you called or were in distress? What if your advisor's primary objective was to ensure your safety? An advisor who desired more than anything that you reach your appointed destination. Just as the OnStar system can be installed in nearly all of GM's new automobiles, we have the option of having the Holy Spirit live inside our hearts. The Holy Spirit is the agent promised to believers by Christ. It is through the Holy Sprit that we stay connected to Christ.

Help from On High

The writer of the epistle to the Hebrews explains the vital necessity of having an expert advisor and advocate as we journey through life. Moreover, the writer does not suggest just any advisor. The writer specifically directs us to Jesus Christ who is described as our high priest. In order to appreciate the writer's position we must understand the context of the letter. The letter was written to believers who were descendents of the nation of Israel. We learn a great many things about God from His dealings with the nation of Israel that are intended to serve as an example.

Under God's original covenant with the nation of Israel, God selected certain individuals to serve as priests. It is important to understand that priests were not chosen because of how they lived; rather the fact that they were chosen dictated their lifestyle. While human error and unnecessary traditions have detracted from a proper understanding of the role of a priest, God's Word defines His objective clearly. Priests were set apart by God to represent the nation or people before God. Their primary function was to offer sacrifices that atoned for sin. Sin separates people from God. Thus priests were essentially responsible for keeping men connected to God. Inasmuch as the Old Testament sacrifices were imperfect and symbolic, the priests of that day could not effectively keep men connected to God. This is why the Old Testament, also known as the Old Covenant, is perfected through the ministry of Jesus Christ.

The writer of Hebrews alludes to the new covenant that God offers to all men through the perfect sacrifice of His Son Jesus Christ. Upon completing His ministry in the earth Jesus has taken on the role of High Priest in heaven. By that, the scripture means that Jesus Himself represents all of mankind before God. He is an advocate who pleads our case as we work through the challenges of life, and He is an advisor that provides direction through His written and spoken word. As the writer of Hebrews says, we must stay connected to God and never stop trusting Him. When we allow His Spirit to live inside of us, we can confidently ask for His grace and His mercy, having assurance that we will receive His assistance whenever we need it.

Lost and Found

"The former priests, on the one hand, existed in greater numbers because they were prevented by death from continuing, but Jesus, on the other hand, because He continues forever, holds His priesthood permanently. Therefore He is able also to save forever those who draw near to God through Him, since He always lives to make intercession for them." Hebrews 7:23-25 NASB

When traveling to an unfamiliar destination or along an unfamiliar route, what phrase do you least want to hear or utter? While there may be some debate on this topic, my guess is the phrase "I'm lost" is high on that list. There are few circumstances that cause as much discomfort or stress as being lost. If there is one thing we all have in common, it is our aversion to the helplessness we feel when we can't find our way. This basic human trait explains why so many people are frustrated with their current life circumstances. From a spiritual standpoint, most people are knowingly or unknowingly lost on the road of life. This is why Jesus of Nazareth often described His ministry as an effort to seek and save those who are lost (Luke 19:10).

Let's consider an everyday example. Have you ever lost your way traveling to an unfamiliar destination? If you are a frequent traveler, you have probably gotten turned around on more occasions than you care to admit. I am a fairly methodical person so I typically go through great lengths to guard against getting lost. Whether charting my trip in advance or getting detailed directions, I diligently prepare. Especially when traveling to an unfamiliar destination.

As we all know, traveling conditions are unpredictable. So despite my best efforts I have gotten lost on more than one occasion. On one particular occasion, I was traveling with a friend to visit some folks in western Illinois. We'd gotten directions verbally and though we'd never been to our destination, we felt comfortable that we could easily find our way. The trip was largely uneventful until we unwittingly missed a landmark and subsequent turn. It's interesting to note that we often intuitively realize when we are lost before the facts materialize. It's that strange feeling that you have been going too long or that your current locale simply doesn't feel right. This is the state that we found ourselves in.

There seems to be a relatively predictable series of attitudes that one exhibits when lost. The first of these is denial. For some inexplicable reason this is particularly common among male travelers like my friend and me. Although the distance didn't seem quite right and our intuition suggested we'd erred, we were convinced that we were on the proper course. We reasoned this despite the fact that we were traveling to an unfamiliar destination. Social scientists refer to this human trait as overconfidence. Overconfidence resulted in an additional fifteen miles down the wrong course. This was a distance that we'd ultimately have to retrace.

The second attitude that sets in is frustration. Frustration is the natural successor to denial. Once the truth sets in that you're lost, you face an interesting predicament. Your best thinking has gotten you to where you are and you realize that you don't have the right answer. That's the situation we encountered on our trip to western Illinois. Once we crossed the border into Iowa, we knew we'd missed our destination. Naturally, we turned around, but we were frustrated because we were unsure of what we'd do next. This was long before the times of the ubiquitous cell phone, so we couldn't simply reach out and touch someone.

The third attitude that generally sets in is fear. The fear may develop on a number of levels. It can simply be a concern that you will not arrive at your destination in a timely fashion or it can be a grave concern for your personal safety. We intuitively know that knowledge of where we're headed is vital to ensuring safe travel. It is very difficult to guard against potential hazards when you are uncertain of where you are headed. Given we were two city kids in the middle of dark farm country, our fear factor was skewed toward the measure for personal safety. We quickly realized that it was time for us to seek assistance. After stops at several service stations, we were able to piece together enough travel advice to make our way to our destination. Maybe this experience among others is why the OnStar commercials were appealing to me.

Connected to High Places

This trip down memory lane serves as a useful anecdote as we consider the experience of traveling through life. Far too often we find ourselves misdirected or without direction altogether as we make important decisions in life. At the time of my trip to western Illinois, vehicles were not equipped with the sophisticated technology that they have today. Whether OnStar or a host of comparable technologies, we have the opportunity to better equip ourselves when we take to the open road. We have an even greater source of direction and safety as it pertains to our spiritual lives. The Word of God took on human form to, among other things, serve as our perfect example and guide. The testimony of His life serves as a road map for us to follow as we similarly make our way through life.

Christ does not simply provide us with His written Word as a road map. He desires that His Word come alive in us and that we benefit from a personal relationship with Him. The writer of Hebrews expounds on this relationship, referring again to Jesus as our High Priest. He explains that Jesus is not a temporary advisor. He is permanently seated in heavenly places making intercession for those who have accepted Him as Lord. Jesus takes great pleasure in this current ministry as He looks forward to rewarding faithful travelers when they reach their ultimate destination.

So how does this heavenly arrangement work? I'm glad someone asked! We must start with a principle that we established earlier in the text. Each of us has the freedom to make our own choices. This is also true as it relates to our relationship with God. In a manner of speaking, we each have the option to choose whether we want God's Spirit to dwell within us. However, it is only through the Holy Spirit that we are closely connected to God. We can opt to go it alone or we can submit to Christ's authority and receive His Spirit.

I've often held that well-meaning people misconstrue God's message with religious rhetoric and manmade traditions. God has desired one thing from man throughout the course of history. His desire is for true fellowship. His Word plainly tells us that this fellowship can only come through faith in Jesus Christ, the express image of God. Jesus rightly claimed to be the only way to true salvation. People wrongly contend that this understanding of salvation is exclusionary. However, that is totally unfounded and untrue. Christ's offer for salvation is wonderfully inclusive and transcends ethnicity, nationality, culture, and religion. Christ invites all who truly desire to enjoy a lasting relationship with Him.

The truths set forth in the Bible tell us how to maintain a healthy relationship with the true living God. These truths also serve as concrete principles to guide us to our God ordained destination in life. In order to enjoy God's grace and guidance we must do three basic things. We must accept Jesus Christ as our Lord and follow the example that He set before us. This allegiance requires that we obey His Word. Secondly, we must receive the gift of His indwelling Spirit, which helps us along the way. Those who receive God's Spirit and commune with Him must be holy for God is holy (1 Pet. 1:15). Practically, this means that we must live in a manner that is consistent with God's character. Finally, we must do the necessary things that keep us in fellowship with God. This includes seeking His will when we make decisions in life.

The Holy Spirit in effect works like the Global Positioning System technology that is the foundation for OnStar and the other vehicle systems found in modern vehicles. Global Positioning Systems literally use satellites that orbit in space to pinpoint a vehicle's location at any time of day or night. With this capability a driver can receive directions or assistance whenever he or she makes the conscious decision to simply ask. Christ is ready and willing to intervene. In fact, it is His primary occupation. However, it is up to you to ask.

Maybe you're currently in a situation where you've lost your way. Maybe you've consciously made a wrong turn and are having trouble getting back on course. Maybe you are figuratively stranded on the road of life due to unforeseen circumstances. I've personally had both experiences of being lost. Whatever your present situation, you can take comfort in the fact that your heavenly Father is just a breath away. If you will humble yourself and ask for His assistance, He will meet you wherever you are. Moreover, He will upgrade you with a fresh refilling of His Spirit and get you back on the right course to achieve your destiny.

●

Part
4

Finish
Your
Course

"No, dear brothers and sisters, I am still not all I should be, but I am focusing all my energies on this one thing: Forgetting the past and looking forward to what lies ahead, I strain to reach the end of the race and receive the prize for which God, through Christ Jesus, is calling us up to."
Philippians 3:13-14, NLT

Two weeks ago my wife and I were enjoying a quiet Saturday afternoon, which is rare these days. I turned on the television to get an update on college football scores when the telecast of the Ironman triathlon competition caught our attention. The Ironman triathlon competition is a grueling endurance race that comprises a 2.4-mile swim, a 112-mile bike ride, and a 26.2-mile run. For those who are counting, the run is equivalent to a marathon by itself. While any of the three segments that comprise the race are challenging, the combination of the three demands incredible physical stamina and mental toughness.

The Ironman competition was born out of a debate by a group of sports enthusiasts who wanted to determine who was the most physically fit among runners, swimmers, and cyclists. The group planned to settle the debate by combining the three existing long-distance events in each discipline that were being held in Hawaii at the time. With a little planning and less fanfare, the first Ironman triathlon took place in Hawaii in 1978. Over the years the event has grown in popularity. The main competition held in Hawaii attracts over fifteen hundred contestants. Taken together with qualifying events across the globe, the Ironman triathlon competitions draw people from every imaginable walk of life.

We were enthralled by the incredible personal stories of the Ironman contestants. We were introduced to schoolteachers, stockbrokers, wealthy business owners, and recent college graduates. The field included a competitor with a debilitating disease that would confine him to a wheelchair within a year. The field also included a grandmother who after twenty years was still competing at the tender age of seventy-eight. As we listened to their stories, we quickly realized a very important truth. The vast majority of the participants were not competing against their fellow contestants. Instead they were each running an individual race. And while each contestant ran his or her race, they did share the same goal: to successfully finish their course. For upon completion, the contestant joined an exclusive league of extraordinary individuals who don the title of "Ironman" or "Ironwoman."

As we watched the footage of those determined men and women crossing the finish line, we could not help but be moved by their accomplishment. As grueling as the race must have been, the actual event only tells part of the story. The field was predominantly made up of weekend warriors as opposed to professional athletes. Therefore most of the field had to prepare for the event while managing their varied professional and personal responsibilities. The discipline and sacrifice required to achieve such a feat is incredible. We were also moved by the tremendous outpouring of joy and emotion expressed as the contestants crossed the finish line. Completing the race had a wonderfully unique meaning to each contestant.

While I may never compete in an Ironman triathlon, watching the event reinforced several important life lessons. The spirit of what I've learned is captured by the Apostle Paul in his letter to the Philippians. Paul is quite transparent in his communication, and it is clear that maturity and life experience had humbled him. While Paul readily admitted his shortcomings, he refused to let them deter him from the course set before him. Instead he focused all of his energy and effort on the successful completion of his course. He naturally encountered highs and lows along the way. However, he exercised humility during the highs and learned to be content during the lows. Through all things he fought and endured to the finish. Like present-day Ironmen, Paul had but one goal: the finish line. Paul knew that with Christ as his example and the Holy Spirit as his guide that he had what it took to persevere to the end.

Paul's impassioned words have often caused me to reflect on my own life. At times I falter and am disappointed by my actions. At other times I'm reminded of troubled memories from my past. Nevertheless, I fight to see myself from God's perspective and keep my eyes on the prize of eternal life. Though every day does not go as I hope or plan, the Holy Spirit strengthens me to keep pressing toward the finish. My desire is to see my Lord at the end of the race and hear His commendation for a course well run. Like Paul, I am driven by the vital necessity of finishing. For it is in finishing that I can proudly proclaim eternally that I am a son of God and a joint heir with Christ.

Remember that Christ's offer is inclusive. Each of us has the opportunity to reign with Him in eternity. However, in order to receive your prize and your rightful place in God's eternal kingdom, you must finish your course. Bear in mind that the course was designed for you and that you are especially equipped for your journey. This brings to mind the lyrics of an old gospel song. The writer noted that the race of life is not necessarily given to the swift or the strong but that the victor is the individual who endures until the end. The final section of the book is meant to encourage you to finish your course through the power of God's Spirit. The Apostle Paul and a multitude of others can testify to the truth that you will win if you don't quit.

●

Chapter

13

Checkpoints

"So we have continued praying for you ever since we first heard about you.
We ask God to give you a complete understanding of what he wants to do in
your lives, and we ask him to make you wise with spiritual wisdom.
Then the way you live will always honor and please the Lord, and you will
continually do good, kind things for others."
Colossians 1:9-11, NLT

The terrorist attacks that occurred on September 11, 2001, irrevocably
changed many aspects of American life. In the immediate aftermath of the
tragedy, the Federal Aviation Administration made an unprecedented decision to ban all air traffic in U.S. airspace with the exception of military air-
craft. On a given day, there are approximately 87,000 flights in the United
States. About 30,000 of these are commercial, with the rest made up of private, taxi, cargo, and military flights. The ban, which lasted for several days,
revealed the necessity and vulnerability of the air transportation system in
the United States. This attack on the commercial airlines ushered in signifi-

cant changes in the country's approach to and administration of transportation security.

Shortly after the tragedies, the Transportation Security Administration (TSA) was formed. This U.S. agency is a component of the Department of Homeland Security and is responsible for safekeeping of the nation's transportation systems. The stated mission of the TSA is to protect the nation's transportation systems, ensuring freedom of movement for people and commerce. With state, local, and regional partners, the agency oversees security for the highways, railroads, buses, mass transit systems, ports, and U.S. airports. This is a significant task for which the agency employs over fifty thousand people across the country.

As you might expect and as any frequent flyer knows, the most noticeable presence of the TSA is in the arena of airline security. TSA officials and personnel are responsible for security and passenger screening in most of the nation's nearly 4,500 airports. As a frequent flyer myself, I have become well acquainted with the agency's processes and procedures. Most notably, I have become all too familiar with the passenger screening processes that have been implemented at virtually all commercial airports.

Security checkpoints at airports are hardly a new concept. They are a hallmark of a properly functioning airline system. Moreover, checkpoints are employed in many aspects of the nation's transportation system. Whether it is a sobriety checkpoint set up to guard against intoxicated drivers or an immigration checkpoint set up to control access to the nation's borders, checkpoints are an important tool used by government authorities. While these checkpoints are established explicitly to guard the safety of the citizens who utilize the transportation system, travelers often fail to appreciate the vital role that checkpoints play.

For example, have you ever been driving home late at night or early in the morning and been delayed because highway patrolmen had set up a security checkpoint? I'm going to go out on a limb and guess that your first thought was not "thank goodness these kind folks are out here ensuring the roadways are safe for me and my family." More often than not we find ourselves agitated because the quick check has added two or three minutes to our commute. Rarely do we consider how many dangerous drivers have been taken off of the road or, better still, how many potential offenders have been deterred by these protective measures.

Admittedly, I've been guilty of the same type of attitude when it comes to flying. For most of my professional career I have been a regular business traveler. The two things that I enjoy least about flying are airport traffic and security screening. Prior to 9/11 I largely viewed security screening as an inconvenience. As much as possible I would schedule my flights during nonpeak hours to avoid long lines at checkpoints. Like so many other weary travelers, I wanted the microwave version of airport security. It wasn't that I didn't value my security. The fact of the matter was I simply did not have an appreciation for the potential risks.

My attitude toward flying was somewhat indicative of my attitude toward life. We are often so focused on our personal agenda or preoccupied by the business of life that we do not appreciate what's most important. If our ultimate objective is safe arrival, then we should have a greater appreciation for the actions that ensure safe travel. When we view things from God's perspective as opposed to our limited point of view, our attitude is greatly altered. Not only do we exercise greater patience, but we make better decisions in life.

The Apostle Paul conveyed similar sentiments to believers in Colosse. In his letter to the Colossians, Paul focused his attention on encouraging the young church in their pursuit of a new way of life. Paul prayed that his readers would attain understanding and wisdom from God regarding His will for their lives. Paul knew that through the leading of the Holy Spirit that they would be able to find their way in life. He also was confident that the Holy Spirit would empower them to live in a manner that was pleasing to God. Paul's communication effectively served as a checkpoint to ensure their safe progression. Like the Colossians, we also need checkpoints to help ensure our progress and safety as we travel to our destination.

Seeking Things Above

"Set your affection on things above, not on things on the earth."
Colossians 3:2, KJV

The Apostle Paul's letter to the Colossians provides a wealth of advice for living a life inspired by the Holy Spirit. One of the more profound insights that Paul provides is with respect to the traveler's perspective. Paul encourages his readers to set their sights on things above as opposed to earthly things. If we endeavor to rise above our current reality, we have to have a renewed focus. This new lifestyle does come with its challenges. As an unknown author once remarked, "The joy of flying is so often preceded by the fear of falling." When we set our heart on things above, we must be prepared to make the necessary sacrifices to reach our destination.

When we select air transportation as our means of travel, we are in essence setting our sights on things above. Air travel physically connects us to people and resources in every corner of the world. It enables business and commerce never dreamed of a century ago. Air travel also gives us access to parts of the world that we may have previously only read or dreamed about. Yet with its many benefits, air travel has inherent risks and safety concerns. As such, the TSA provides useful advice for travelers who take advantage of the commercial airline network in the United States. The TSA also provides practical tips for those of us who endeavor to set our sights on things above.

Travel Tip #1: Pack Wisely

The first piece of advice that the TSA provides relates to the preparation for your trip. The agency encourages travelers to pack wisely. Travelers are responsible for packing their own luggage. In this way, they are well acquainted with the items they are traveling with. Travelers should pack lightly, only taking necessary items. The TSA also provides guidance with respect to permissible items. Certain items that the traveler may perceive as harmless may be inappropriate for air travel. Travelers are responsible for keeping abreast of the rules that apply to luggage as conditions and associated regulations may change.

Recall from earlier in the text that the writer of Hebrews encourages readers to lay aside anything that would hinder their progress on the road of life (Heb. 12:1). The road of life presents varied challenges that require us to act prudently and wisely. As such, we must rid ourselves of negative attitudes, emotional baggage, and sinful desires, none of which are intended to accompany us on our trip. Through His Spirit, God relieves us of any unnecessary burdens that we carry as we make our way through life. Whether the application is literal or figurative, packing wisely is the only way to travel.

Travel Tip #2: Identify Yourself

While luggage is certainly important, the most essential item a traveler must possess is the appropriate identification. Without proper ID, the traveler's trip is over before it begins. If a U.S. citizen is traveling within the United States, a driver's license or another valid picture ID issued by a government agency is generally required. If a U.S. citizen is traveling internationally, a valid passport issued by the U.S. government is required to board the flight and ultimately to enter a visiting country.

In Paul's letter to the Ephesians he assures us that all believers regardless of nationality or ethnicity have equal access to the Father in heaven. In fact, Paul refers to believers as citizens of God's kingdom (Eph. 2:19). With this citizenship come certain privileges, including the right to move freely throughout the kingdom. The indwelling Spirit is the agent by which we actualize our rights as citizens. It is also the agent that effectively identifies us as citizens. We must receive the Holy Spirit into our hearts and affirm that He is with us wherever we go. The Holy Spirit validates our citizenship in God's kingdom and our standing as joint heirs with Christ.

Travel Tip #3: Arrive Early

Once your luggage is packed and you have proper identification, it's time to head for the airport. One of the most frequent refrains that travelers hear from the TSA admonishes them to arrive early. Given the significant volume of travelers that fly commercially and the increased security threats, the security screening process can be time consuming. The effectiveness of the process is compromised when airline and TSA personnel have to deal with frustrated passengers. As the saying goes, the best defense is a good offense. To ensure that you make your scheduled departure, it is advised that you take the simple precaution of arriving early. This simple tradeoff will not only help ensure your departure, but it will generally reduce your level of stress.

The Apostle Paul understood the necessity of making tradeoffs. Whether it was a sacrifice of time or resources, Paul was always willing to do what was necessary to reach his destination. Paul's second letter to the Corinthians effectively captures his attitude in this regard. Paul viewed the inconveniences he encountered as light and temporary (2 Cor. 4:17). More importantly, they simply paled in comparison to reaching his eternal destiny. His keen focus on his destination enabled him to make the necessary tradeoffs and sacrifices to complete his journey.

Travel Tip #4: Guard Your Belongings

If you've spent any time in the airport, you are very familiar with a particular announcement. Travelers are reminded repeatedly to never leave their luggage unattended. Firstly, we must consider the reason we pack luggage to begin with. The items in our luggage are intended to be useful on our trip. As such, we should protect those items so that they don't become lost or stolen. The misappropriation of our luggage can impair our trip or derail it altogether, depending on the necessity of the items packed.

In Paul's letter to the Corinthians he also makes mention of precious treasure that God entrusts us with on our journey (2 Cor. 4:7). This vital treasure is our knowledge of God's Word and the good news concerning His eternal kingdom. This message is vitally important because it helps guide us to our ultimate destination. Moreover, it is given to us by God to share with others everywhere that we travel. Paul describes our bodies as the vessels or containers used to transport our precious cargo. Given the vulnerable and perishable nature of our vessels, they must be protected at all times. We must stay connected to God through His Spirit so that we are under His divine protection at all times. Additionally, we must be spiritually aware so that we are careful stewards over the things that God entrusts to our care.

Travel Tip #5: Beware of Strangers

Airport security also advises travelers to beware of strangers. Specifically, we are advised never to accept packages from strangers. While it may seem innocent, accepting packages from strangers can be hazardous to our health and the health of fellow travelers. Evildoers intent on causing harm to you or others may try to use you as an unsuspecting host of dangerous items if you do not keep your wits about you. Something that may seem as innocent as temporarily taking custody of an item while the person purports to run an errand could prove to be an unwise decision. We must be more circumspect than ever given the strategies that individuals with malicious intent employ.

The writer of Hebrews cautions readers not to be led astray by strangers with seductive philosophy and foreign teaching (Heb. 13:9). He instead encourages his readers to rely on God's Word, which is of proven value. Moreover, readers should receive their instruction from individuals whose conduct and actions they have personally observed. This advice is critical in today's society as false teachers are found everywhere from bookstand to pulpit. While many helpful sources of advice are available, we must be careful that any instruction we accept is consistent with God's Word. God's Word is proven and its fundamental principles never change. The Holy Spirit enables us to properly discern truth from error. However, our job is to guard our hearts by rejecting foreign and potentially dangerous influences.

Travel Tip #6: Be Respectful

The TSA respectfully asks that travelers learn to appreciate the fact that security personnel are responsible for ensuring our safety. It may seem surprising that the TSA has to ask passengers to exercise common courtesy. However, as a frequent traveler I've observed that respect for these service professionals is increasingly uncommon. Travelers are often irritable and at times downright offensive. This is confounding given the fact that airline and TSA personnel are charged with the daunting task of ensuring the safety of millions of passengers every day. As travelers we can show our appreciation by dutifully following instructions and cooperating with all requests. We can also demonstrate our appreciation by understanding when inevitable delays occur.

The writer of Hebrews similarly encourages his readers to respect the authority of their spiritual leaders (Heb. 13:17). Spiritual leaders are responsible for watching over us and are accountable to God for the manner in which they carry out their responsibilities. God places them in our lives to encourage our progress and to work on His behalf to help ensure our safe travel. When we humble ourselves and submit to the teaching and mentorship of godly spiritual leaders, our Father in heaven assures us that it works for our benefit.

Travel Tip #7: Stay Alert

The final tip regards shared accountability, or doing our part with regard to safety. While the TSA expends great time, energy, and resources to ensure the safety of the traveling public, their efforts alone could never be sufficient. Each traveler has a personal responsibility to contribute to the safety of all travelers. To that end, the TSA reminds travelers to be alert at all times. We are encouraged to immediately report any suspicious activity to airport security. It is often the courageous efforts of the traveling public that enable the TSA to achieve their mission of ensuring safe passage for millions of travelers every day.

In Paul's first epistle to the Corinthians he concludes with a very heartfelt admonishment to guide them along the unpredictable road of life. He tells them to be on alert and stand firm in the faith. He encourages them to be courageous and strong and to show love toward their fellow men (1 Cor. 16:13). The road of life is challenging. However, it is the requisite challenges that bring out the best in us. The journey that God has set before us requires every bit of faith and determination we can muster and more. However, we are assured of a successful journey when the Holy Spirit assists us along the way.

•

Roadblocks

"I have been constantly on the move. I have been in danger from rivers, in danger from bandits, in danger from my own countrymen, in danger from Gentiles; in danger in the city, in danger in the country, in danger at sea; and in danger from false brothers. I have labored and toiled and have often gone without sleep; I have known hunger and thirst and have often gone without food; I have been cold and naked. Besides everything else, I face daily the pressure of my concern for all the churches."
2 Corinthians 11:26-28, NIV

It is through the epistles authored by the Apostle Paul, many of which we have highlighted in the text, that we gain great insight into his faith and his life's journey. Paul's second letter to the church at Corinth was written during the latter stages of what is referred to as his third missionary journey. Nearly two decades had transpired since his life-changing experience on Damascus road. His obedience to the call of God had enabled him to touch countless lives through his teaching and living example.

The second epistle to the Corinthians is probably the most autobiographical of Paul's letters. Paul was generally careful to avoid boasting about himself because his life's work was to lead others to Christ. Nevertheless, constant personal attacks provoked Paul to respond in a more personal way. In his letter to the Corinthians Paul defends his character and his ministry by providing an intimate perspective of the ministry to which he dedicated his life. It is from this perspective that we gain key insights into the challenges and triumph that we face as we travel toward our ultimate destination in life.

In one memorable section of his letter, Paul describes specific challenges he'd faced on his many journeys. Paul's challenges included constant and difficult travel, physical infirmities and attacks, emotional distress, and financial hardship. He by no means enjoyed a life of luxury. In fact, he noted that he often went without food, drink, or a comfortable place to lay his head. Furthermore, Paul was in constant danger coming from every direction. Bandits were a common threat as he often traveled with few companions. Foreigners and fellow countrymen alike often opposed his ministry and sought to injure him emotionally and physically. He also encountered individuals he described as false brothers who feigned a belief in God yet sought to do him harm.

At first glance, it is hard to appreciate Paul's experience. This account hardly sounds like the testimony of a man under the divine guidance and protection of God. However, we must come to appreciate our experiences from God's perspective. God fully knows why He created us and how He designed us. When we fully entrust our lives to Him, He carefully choreographs our journey so that we can fulfill our assignments and develop into our true selves. Paul learned a humbling lesson which we all must learn. Along the road of life, you will inevitably run into road blocks.

A roadblock is an obstruction that prevents passage on a particular route. The obstruction may be a result of happenstance, such as a fallen tree caused by a violent storm. The obstruction may be intentional, such as a barricade set up by road transportation authorities. Figuratively speaking, a roadblock is a situation or condition that makes it difficult to make progress or achieve an objective. It is important to note that whether we are speaking figuratively or literally, roadblocks are virtually always temporary.

Paul faced many roadblocks that made achieving his goals difficult. Paul undoubtedly questioned why God allowed certain challenges in his life. After all, it's frustrating to run into an obstruction when you are traveling down what you believe is the right path. God allows adversity in our lives so that we learn patient endurance. It is this quality that enables us to persevere until we reach our final destination. Unfortunately, many people perceive temporary obstructions as permanent barriers. This mindset causes people to give up at the time when they should look up.

Have you ever been traveling in a car and unexpectedly run into a roadblock? What did you do? I suspect in nearly every case you persevered to your destination. Though you weren't able to continue down that particular route, the roadblock did not change your destination. Why would it? Life's journey is quite similar in this respect. Though we may encounter situations or conditions that hinder our progress, we should never allow these impediments to stop our journey or change our destination. Roadblocks are temporary, but our destination is eternal. Since our destination never changes, neither should our resolve.

What should you do when you encounter a roadblock as you journey through life? In my opinion it is a clear signal that we need to seek guidance from God so that we can proceed along an alternate route. Notice that the qualification involves seeking God. While it is important that we do not give up, it is equally important that we do not lean on our own understanding. A roadblock does not signify the wrong destination. It also does not necessarily signify that you made the wrong choice, so you can stop beating yourself up. It does however signify that you need to proceed in a different direction. If your ultimate destination is determined by God, it makes perfect sense that you would consult Him when it's time for you to change course.

Let the Weak Say I Am Strong

"And He has said to me, "My grace is sufficient for you, for power is perfected in weakness." Most gladly, therefore, I will rather boast about my weaknesses, so that the power of Christ may dwell in me. Therefore I am well content with weaknesses, with insults, with distresses, with persecutions, with difficulties, for Christ's sake; for when I am weak, then I am strong."
2 Corinthians 12:9-10, NASB

Paul's unique gifts, education, and experience allowed God to use him in extraordinary ways. Paul received incredible revelations from God regarding things past and things to come. Paul explained that God had an interesting way of making sure he remained humble. Paul describes what he referred to as a thorn in his flesh. Though many commentators believe that Paul is alluding to a physical ailment, the language is figurative and more aptly describes the constant persecution and opposition Paul endured.

It is important to note that Paul recognized that the roadblock that he faced was permitted by God. In fact, Paul writes that he earnestly sought the Lord on three different occasions to remove the persecutions he faced. It is difficult for us to appreciate the wisdom of God in allowing the circumstances of life to "buffet" us as Paul exclaimed. However, this is exactly what God does. For reasons that we later learn to understand and appreciate, God is glorified through our weaknesses.

In response to Paul's pleas, God offers the following response. God explained to Paul that His grace was all that Paul required. Paul wanted God to remove his opposition when in fact God desired that he overcome his opposition. Though Paul felt weak due to his opposition, this was the situation in which God could be glorified through his life. As Paul learned, power or ability is often perfected in weakness. Paul himself and not his opposition posed the greatest threat to his journey. Therefore God permitted roadblocks or opposition in Paul's life so that he would constantly rely on Him. It was through his weakness that Paul learned to truly trust God.

Paul learned his lesson well. Instead of boasting in his gifts or his strengths, he stated that he boasted in his weaknesses. Paul believed his weaknesses were evidence of the power of God working in him. When he endured insults, calamities, and persecutions for Christ's sake, the inner working of the Holy Spirit became evident to those around him. The roadblocks Paul faced served several purposes. Firstly, they helped expose his weaknesses and allowed him to grow. Secondly, they kept him humble and allowed God to continue to use him. Finally, they allowed Paul to overcome in a manner that brought praise and glory to God.

Maybe you've encountered roadblocks during your journey that you've never come to terms with. Maybe you are currently facing persecution or opposition that is impeding your progress. Without guidance from God, roadblocks can be discouraging and even defeating. However, you must take courage in knowing that God is glorified through your weakness. God desires to build you up in every area of your life. Moreover, He will lead you when you encounter life's inevitable roadblocks. As Paul learned, the key is humility. God will be glorified through your life and you will persevere to your destination as long as you continue to trust Him.

Risky Business

Though I've encountered many roadblocks in my life, some of my most challenging relate to my entrepreneurial endeavors. Although I've always had a bit of an entrepreneurial spirit, the opportunity to start a business came somewhat unexpectedly. I'd pitched one of my closest friends on the prospect of co-authoring a book project. My thought was that we would author a two-part series by each writing one of the components. This unconventional idea opened a new chapter in my life. My partner suggested that we publish the books ourselves, which led us into our first business venture.

Starting a business, even a small one, is an exhilarating experience. Since we were both married and working full-time jobs, the small venture consumed our spare time. We were long on ideas and short on capital, which led to our first roadblock. This may surprise you, but banks are not lining up to provide financing to upstart authors and publishers. However, we persevered and eventually found a bank that provided modest financing once we pledged some items for security. With manuscripts and limited capital in hand, we went about the process of publishing and marketing our books.

Early on, our optimism ran high. We worked diligently to get our books placed in stores and market them whenever and wherever possible. It is at this point that the roadblocks came more frequently. As unknown authors, it was difficult to get shelf space or air time. While a number of stores locally and nationally carried the books, many stores were simply not interested in our untested product. We attempted to market the books at conferences and expos. However, these efforts were often met with cool responses. We also attempted to market our books directly to churches and other faith-based organizations. However, we were an unknown commodity and our efforts often fell on deaf ears. Our lower than expected sales ensured that our cash reserves were depleted relatively quickly.

Bruised but not defeated we began to ponder the next steps for our business. We'd gotten a good deal of exposure to the Christian retail industry while marketing our books. This experience came into play in our next entrepreneurial foray. A well-known Christian retailer was exiting the retail business and was looking to sell a store that was literally in our back yard. We surprised many people in the industry when we negotiated and closed the deal with the parent company. Through this transaction we were catapulted into the Christian retail business. The opportunity seemed heaven sent. We were further encouraged by the fact that we were able to employ innovative financing and close the transaction by pledging the remaining assets of our declining publishing business. We essentially purchased the store with no money down.

We quickly went about learning the business with intense focus. It was exciting to roll up our sleeves and take on the challenge of reviving a faltering business. Through God's grace and my partner's operational expertise, we stemmed the business losses and got the business to break even in less than a year. I'd love to declare victory but the reality was that it was time for the next roadblock. We'd decided to host a Christian concert. It seemed like a good way to improve our financial position with the additional benefit of marketing the store. We never anticipated the difficulties that we would encounter in selling all the concert seats.

To make a long story short, we had to convert our ticketed concert to a free event. This was a very difficult decision that we made in light of very underwhelming ticket sales. We felt that we could salvage a marketing success with a packed house for the event. From a publicity standpoint, the concert was a success. Free is a price that quickly clears a market. However, the event proved to be nothing short of a financial body blow to our immature business. As proprietors, my partner and I shouldered virtually all of the loss. We literally had purchased the most expensive seats in the house. This proved to be a defining moment for us personally and professionally. It's challenging to praise God in the midst of difficult circumstances. However, sometimes that's all you can do.

Nothing Should Stand in Your Way

I will save you the details of our numerous business travails and simply sum it up by saying that we've had our fair share of challenges. Some of them were the result of economic conditions beyond our control. Some were the result of decisions we made. Others, I suspect, were God's way of teaching us valuable lessons about ourselves and about life. With every roadblock we have faced, we've grown a little wiser and a little stronger. Most importantly, we have increasingly learned to seek direction from God.

I sometimes ponder my decision to venture into the retail business. Prior to our purchase of the store I never had an interest in owning a retail business. While there are a great many things that I learned through the experience, the unpredictable nature of the business taught me the most. Our five-year stint in the retail business was a roller-coaster ride, presenting one challenge after another. Yet while most businesses fail within the first year, we survived and at times thrived. The key to past and future success is the ability to adapt. When we faced a roadblock, we simply changed course as opposed to giving up.

The lessons I learned in the retail business have broader application as I navigate the road of life. Not only do we encounter twists and turns in life, but at times a roadblock stands in our way. We must accept that God has allowed it and that it will ultimately work out in our favor. Roadblocks are ultimately life's way of reminding us that God is in charge. They generally signal a needed change of direction and more importantly they signal our need to seek guidance from God. If we allow God's Spirit to empower us in our times of weakness, then no roadblock will ever keep us from our God-ordained destination.

●

Chapter

15

Rest Stops

"Let us not lose heart in doing good,
for in due time we will reap if we do not grow weary."
Galatians 6:9, NASB

My undergraduate college years were a very important time in my life. Attending school nearly one thousand miles from home broadened my overall experience. Because I'd seldom ventured outside of my city of birth, my initial road trips to the university were fascinating . After driving down to school with me following my first semester, my father decided that it was time to let my friends and I make the long drive to school ourselves. Though I'm sure my mother had a fair bit of concern, my parents realized it was part of my maturation process in life.

Being from a large city, it took a bit of time for me to get accustomed to traveling through the rural parts of the country. At this stage of my life I find the scenery relaxing, but as a young college student I found it unnerving. The trip generally took us about seventeen hours. Our objective was always to complete the journey with as few stops as possible. We were in unfamiliar territory so we preferred to stick to the course and leave little opportunity for delays. As any traveler knows, it's tough to be confined to a vehicle for a long period of time. Therefore, rest stops were an inevitable aspect of each trip.

It was during my trips to the university that I became acquainted with rest areas. Rest areas are often located along remote or rural stretches of highway. They provide restroom facilities, telephones, paved parking areas, and fresh drinking water. Traveler information such as posted maps or visitor information is usually available at public rest stops. In addition to public-or government-maintained areas, there are privatized commercial rest areas that offer modern conveniences, such as food courts, recreation centers, and gas stations. Rest areas prove vitally important to the countless travelers that utilize highway systems all over the world.

I can remember numerous occasions where we became fatigued, thirsty, or hungry and needed some relief in order to complete our trip. The information signs identifying the next rest stop were always a welcome sight. During my four years of college, we made numerous trips between home and school. I can hardly remember a trip when we didn't take advantage of one or more rest areas along the way. Though it didn't occur to us at the time, our short layovers were necessary for the safe completion of our travel.

Rest for the Weary

Galatia was an important stop during Paul's first missionary trip. During an extended stay in Galatia, Paul established strong ties to the community and continually looked after the well-being of the local church that he helped establish in the region. Paul was concerned that the Galatians were straying from their faith and subsequently losing their way on the road of life. The instruction that he gives to the young church reflects his heartfelt concerns.

Paul encourages his young travelers not to lose heart or become discouraged. Far too often in life we start out on the right course only to give up prematurely. Misguided philosophy often calls righteous living into question. I'm sure you've heard some version of the refrain "good guys finish last." The problem with this assertion is that the prognosticator doesn't understand the nature of the race. In the great race of life, only godly men and women have a true hope of finishing the race. This is why Paul admonishes his readers never to become weary of doing what is right. It can similarly be said that we can never become discouraged from following the leading of God's Spirit.

In life, the just reward is bestowed on the contestant who endures to the end. This is why Paul says plainly that we will reap if we do not grow weary. It is important to note that Paul is not referring to physical strength. Instead Paul is referring to our state of mind. We must have a resolve to keep pressing toward our destination even if we have to rest along the way. Our reward in life only comes through hard work and sacrifice. Something we will explore in more detail in our final chapter. God knows exactly how much we can bear and will graciously provide opportunities for rest along the way.

A Run in the Park

"For if a man think himself to be something, when he is nothing,
he deceiveth himself. But let every man prove his own work,
and then shall he have rejoicing in himself alone, and not in another.
For every man shall bear his own burden."
Galatians 6:3-5, KJV

It was the summer of 1996 and I was living in New York City. I was working for a Wall Street firm and had settled into my routine of early mornings and long hours. Since most of my waking hours were spent at work, I'd naturally developed friendships with my fellow associates. One of my colleagues talked me into signing up for a popular 5K run held in Central Park. While the event was technically a competition, the primary aim was to raise money for charity. Businesses throughout the city made contributions for each of their employees who entered and subsequently completed the race. Participants could run or walk if they chose. Again, the objective was to finish the race and make a contribution to the greater good.

My colleague and I were young and relatively healthy. However, our sedentary corporate jobs were taking their toll. My colleague viewed the event as an opportunity to support charity as well as an excuse to become more physically fit. He'd been a wrestler throughout his college career but had given up his regular fitness routine, which included running. I similarly had become fairly inactive after my collegiate days full of intramural sports, workouts, and running. In preparation for the event my colleague began jogging several nights per week. He faithfully stuck to his routine during the six weeks leading up to the race.

Though the prospect of getting back into shape seemed appealing, I was less than enthusiastic about hitting the pavement. I convinced myself that I'd resume a regular fitness routine in the not-too-distant future. As for the event, I had little concern. It was just a 5K run. I'd run this distance countless times. As far as I was concerned, I was in adequate shape to complete the course. Although my colleague would update me from time to time on his progress, I was not similarly persuaded to prepare for the race.

The event was held in the early evening on a business day. My colleague and I brought our running gear into work and headed to the race site directly from the office. As fate would have it, it turned out to be one of the hottest days in New York City that year. It was a real scorcher with the temperature reaching the upper nineties. My lack of training was likely only surpassed by my lack of preparation. I had not properly hydrated myself prior to the run nor had I brought water with me to the event.

We arrived at the event just before the race began. My colleague was fairly confident because he'd been preparing for nearly six weeks. He suggested we make our way to the front where the runners were positioned as opposed to the back of the pack with the joggers and walkers. With thousands of participants crowded near the starting line, I suspect the temperature on the ground easily exceeded the hundred-degree mark. We were profusely sweating before the race even began and were anxious to start running. We estimated that we could navigate the course in about twenty-five minutes after which I planned to make a beeline for some refreshments.

The starting gun sounded and off we ran. While we were not attempting to set any records, we ran at a brisk pace. For the first half of the race I kept in stride with my colleague who was certainly much better prepared. About halfway through the course, I felt tightness in my right calf muscle. It was uncomfortable, but I figured I would just endure the pain. We were halfway home and I wasn't going to let my colleague leave me in his wake. Then it happened! All at once I felt severe cramping in both of my legs. The muscle contractions spanned from my calf muscles through my hamstrings and thighs. It felt as if both of my legs were locking up. Ego aside, I simply could not proceed at that point.

Resting on the side of the course, I took deep breaths and stretched until the muscle contractions subsided. Feeling some temporary relief, I decided to continue the race. I figured I would slow my gait, which would enable me to make my way to the end. About a mile down the course I had to stop a second time when I felt cramping in one of my legs. At this resting point I managed to obtain some drinking water. Then I stretched again and completed the race. My colleague finished the course in twenty-six minutes, just shy of our projection. I hobbled across the finish line eight minutes later, regretting my lack of preparation. Though my legs were sore and my ego was bruised, I was able to contribute to the cause by finishing the course.

My competitiveness had caused me to lose sight of why we'd entered the race in the first place. The goal was to raise money in support of a number of charitable organizations. The only thing that could nullify our contribution was failure to complete the course. Given my lack of preparedness and the challenging conditions, it would have been wise to start further back in the pack and run at a more measured pace. Finishing the course was the ultimate objective. Without stopping to recover, I physically would have been unable to finish the race.

Proceed at Your Own Pace

In Paul's letter to the Galatians he cautions against being conceited or prideful. When we rely solely on our intellect or abilities, we ignore our vital need for God's indwelling Spirit. We also ignore our interdependency on others. In doing so, we deceive ourselves and never realize the wonderful experience that God has reserved especially for us. Paul also cautions against comparing ourselves to others. Instead we should take pride in completing the course that God has assigned for us. We need only focus on our own course and examine our own lives. It is through focus and introspection that we learn to appreciate God's grace in our individual lives. We can rejoice knowing that God is working with us and through us. More importantly, we can have confidence that His Spirit will lead us to our ultimate destination.

Paul also reminds us that every individual must bear his or her own load. This does not mean that we will not receive assistance along the way. God not only places individuals in our lives to encourage and assist us, but He expects us to do the same for others. Moreover, God gives us surety in the form of His indwelling Spirit, who is our Helper and Comforter. Paul's words speak to accountability. We are ultimately accountable for the way we conduct ourselves and deploy the natural and spiritual resources God gives us. This is why Paul instructs us to continually examine our work so that our lives are pleasing to God.

My experience on that hot summer day provides a good anecdote for the lessons that Paul conveyed to the Galatians. Youthful pride caused me to run at a pace that I was unable to maintain. As Paul would say, I deceived myself. My confidence should have been a result of faithful preparation and not untested abilities. I also should have kept my focus on the primary goal, which was completing the race. I was accountable for my contributions, and my actions alone would determine whether I reached my destination.

The race of life has many similarities to the event I described. As we've established previously, we all have a common destination. Yet we have different assignments, circumstances, and abilities. Just as we must be careful to stay in our prescribed lane, we must also proceed at our own pace. We cannot become distracted from our most important goals by trying to emulate others. Aesop's timeless fable about the tortoise and the hare teaches the principle of running at one's own pace. This is not to suggest that we cannot learn from the example of others. I certainly should have followed my colleague's example and prepared for the race. Nevertheless, in a foot race or in the great race of life we must each move at our own pace.

In the journey of life, our ultimate goal is to reach God's kingdom. We must faithfully follow the leading of His Spirit and not let our ego drive us to a pace that is unsustainable. When the pressures of life are weighing you down, you may have to pause to renew your strength. An anonymous poet captured it best when he wrote, "rest if you must, but don't quit." Whether you need to stop to gain perspective or seek encouragement because you are feeling low, God ensures that there are safe rest stops along the road of life. He offers all who are weary or burdened a safe place to rest (Matt. 11:28).

16

Toll Roads

"For his Holy Spirit speaks to us deep in our hearts and tells us that we are
God's children. And since we are his children, we will share his treasures—
for everything God gives to his Son, Christ, is ours, too.
But if we are to share his glory, we must also share his suffering.
Yet what we suffer now is nothing compared to the glory he will give us later."
Romans 8:16-18, NLT

Constructed during the Great Depression, the Pennsylvania Turnpike rev-
olutionized automobile travel in the United States. The original roadway,
which was 160 miles long, was considered the first long-distance rural highway. Stretching from Irwin to Middlesex, it was the first roadway in the
United States that had no cross streets, railroad crossings, or traffic lights
over its entire distance. The four-lane highway accommodated all types of
motor vehicles, including buses and trucks. The turnpike was further distinguished by the seven tunnels that were bored through the mountains of
Pennsylvania. This feature enabled direct travel between key localities.

Prior to the opening of the turnpike on October 1, 1940, traveling long distances by motor vehicle was difficult and often discouraged. There were only a small number of super highways of any sort. A trip through the mountains of Pennsylvania was especially challenging with sharp curves and steep grades. Precursors of the turnpike such as U.S. Highway 30 or U.S. Highway 22 were two-lane roads that were built by paving the path of least resistance. Ironically enough, these paths proved quite challenging for travelers to navigate.

The innovative design and construction employed was unheard of prior to the opening of the turnpike. The modest grades and the open four-lane road allowed unrestricted passing except when traveling through the tunnels. This allowed drivers to travel at their own pace, which further enhanced the experience. Given today's modern interstate highway system, it is difficult for U.S. drivers to appreciate the novelty of a trip on the turnpike during those days. However, one might consider the following facts. A trip on the turnpike cut travel time on the 160-mile route from 5.5 hours to about 2.5 hours. The turnpike was considered so innovative that it made the pages of the *Scientific American Journal*. Most notably, the turnpike inspired the development of similar highways all over the nation.

The Pennsylvania Turnpike was distinguished for another important reason. The turnpike was a toll road, which is a roadway on which authorities charge a toll for use. The toll road concept was not new to Pennsylvania authorities. The National Road was developed for stagecoach and foot traffic in the early 1800s. It became the nation's first toll road when government authorities began charging fees for use in the 1830s. Though tolling was an accepted practice by the time the turnpike was constructed, it was not commonly employed by the nation's early highway system. Given the substantial construction and maintenance costs associated with the turnpike, government authorities had to employ an equitable means of funding the project. It seemed only fair that the beneficiaries pay for the privilege of using the roadway.

The Price of Admission

The toll road concept has similar implications as we consider our journey on the road of life. It is Christ's example that makes our quest for eternal life attainable. Jesus is very clear when He proclaims that He is the way, the truth, and the life (John 14:6). The road that He paved was not without great cost. Jesus was bruised, humiliated, and eventually crucified as a ransom for a debt that He did not owe. It was the price of His life that purchased our freedom and paved the road to eternal life. Jesus overcame this world and He encourages us to follow His lead.

It is important to fully understand the nature of Jesus' invitation to follow Him. The term *follow*, which Jesus used in His invitation to prospective disciples, is translated from the Greek word *akoloutheo*. This word has a slightly different meaning than the English word that we are familiar with. The Greek word means to take the same road as another. The idea is not so much to follow behind but more precisely means to join or accompany. When we commit our lives to Christ, we allow His Spirit to guide our decisions. In this way, we are one with Him as we make our way through life.

There is a toll that we must surrender if we choose to take the road that Christ has paved. God's Word instructs us that the disciplined driver on the road of life must forsake his own interests, take up his cross daily, and follow Christ (Luke 9:23). The concept of taking one's cross speaks to the toll or cost. The cross was a vivid and tangible symbol of death, which is the ultimate sacrifice. Jesus sacrificed His life in order to pave the road to eternal life. As such, the toll that is required from us is the sacrifice of our own selfish desires. Just as a toll is routinely collected, God's Word tells us we must bear our cross daily. This means that we must forsake our sinful way of living in order to gain eternal life. A ransomed life is the cost of eternal salvation. Jesus requires nothing more and nothing less.

The Apostle Paul understood the concept of taking up one's cross daily. After all, it was Paul who once wrote that he died daily (1 Cor. 15:31). Paul writes that it is the Holy Spirit who speaks to our hearts, assuring us of our relationship with God. It is this assurance that gives us the inner strength to make our way through life. God has offered us the distinct honor of being part of His royal family and joint heirs with His only begotten Son, Jesus Christ. It is in His manifested kingdom that we will receive our reward and share in His treasures.

Are you willing to do what is necessary to complete your course? This is the question that we inevitably must answer. Paul tells us that if we are to eventually share in Christ's glory, we must first be willing to share in his suffering. This means we will be persecuted, misunderstood, and even mistreated. These are the things we must endure to finish our course. Nevertheless, our ultimate prize is greater than any problems we may encounter in this life. As Paul concluded, nothing we suffer in this life can remotely compare to the reward we will receive when our journey is complete.

Bought with a Price

"And so, dear brothers and sisters, I plead with you to give your bodies to God.
Let them be a living and holy sacrifice – the kind he will accept.
When you think of what he has done for you, is this too much to ask?
Don't copy the behavior and customs of this world, but let God transform you
into a new person by changing the way you think. Then you will know what
God wants you to do, and you will know how good and pleasing and perfect
his will really is." Romans 12:1-2, NLT

Paul's letter to the Romans is believed by many to be his crowning literary work. In the letter he deftly articulates the tenets of his faith in a manner that makes following Christ desirable and achievable. The way that Paul introduces himself to his readers is very telling. His reference to his calling as an apostle or special messenger is preceded by his distinction as a servant of Christ Jesus. The subtleties here should not be overlooked. He is called or chosen to be an apostle. However, he expressly identifies himself as Jesus' servant.

The term *servant* is translated from the Greek word *doulos*, which means bond-servant or slave. The literal definition can refer to a person born or purchased as a slave. The metaphorical definition that Paul employed denotes one who gives himself over to another. The servant is bound to his lord and his purpose is to do the bidding of his lord. Paul's distinction speaks to the attitude of the servant who must set aside his or her own interest. The role of a bond servant would have been clearly understood by his Roman readers. There were certain individuals who were deemed "slaves" of the Emperor of Rome. It is, however, important to note that this was a position of honor for the individual who enjoyed such a relationship with the king. There is a similar implication in Paul's description of his relationship with Christ Jesus.

Paul effectively begs his readers to dutifully pay their toll on the road of life. Paul is very transparent with respect to the cost. He tells his readers that they must give their bodies to God. By this Paul meant that they must dedicate their lives to serving God. He described their prospective lives as a living sacrifice. This implied that they would constantly have to subjugate their will to God's. Paul also explained that this is the only toll that God will accept. It is what can be considered payment-in-kind. He requires our lives inasmuch as He gave His life. Paul contends that the toll not only is reasonable, but it is what we rightly owe God in exchange for all that He is in our lives.

Paul warns his readers not to take shortcuts. Many people are unwilling to pay the required toll yet they want the rewards that come only through serving God. We take shortcuts or ill-advised routes when we mimic the behaviors and attitudes of those who have rejected God's Word. However, these alternative routes ultimately lead to dead ends. Paul admonishes his readers to allow God to radically transform their attitude. This change of attitude can only come through following the leading of His Spirit and faithfully obeying His instructions. Only then will we learn how wonderful His plans are for us.

What You Have to Give

Paul's message began to truly resonate early on in my adult life. Though I'd spent my adolescent and teenage years in church, I'd strayed from this positive influence. Like many others before me, I decided to tackle the road of life on my own. I was successful academically and later professionally as I moved from college to the workforce. Success in these areas gave me a false sense of confidence as I made my way along the road of life. This caused me to measure my self-worth by my accomplishments as opposed to my destiny. After much prompting from God, and a lot of personal introspection, I rededicated my life to Christ.

For some people, the moment of truth comes dramatically. Paul's conversion on Damascus road was a crisis, or decisive moment in his life. Though

I similarly reached a decisive moment in my life, it was not dramatic by any means. It was, however, a clear revelation that occurred through the grace of God. I realized that my life was incomplete. I had given myself over to the behaviors and cares of the world and by my calculation, had little of lasting value to show for it. Jesus' words rang true. What benefit is it to gain temporal things at the risk of losing eternal life? (Mark 8:36) I was lost and my heart was searching for the thing that would make me whole.

Without the Spirit to guide me, I was unconsciously headed in the wrong direction. I was also facing a very crucial dilemma. I knew there was a better way. However, I also knew that I could not find my way on my own. As my father is fond of saying, "No one who is truly lost finds their way home. Someone has to go and rescue the lost." I made a decision at that point that I was tired of leaning on my own understanding. I wanted to experience real joy in this life and the life to come. This type of joy can only be achieved through a personal relationship with God. So with a contrite heart, I humbled myself and asked Jesus to rescue me.

Twelve years have passed since I decided to make my life a living sacrifice. I determined once and for all to surrender my will in exchange for the promise of eternal life. Once I committed my life to Christ, the Holy Spirit filled my heart, becoming my companion and guide. With God's Spirit leading me, I am experiencing life in a whole new way. This new life that I have found in Christ involves personal sacrifice as Paul rightly asserts. However, like Paul, I am fully persuaded that the temporal life that I have surrendered is nothing in comparison to the eternal life that I have gained.

Paul notes in a different letter that we are bought with a price (1 Cor. 6:20). He reminds us that Jesus has not only paid the debt for our sins but has chosen to forget them altogether. Inasmuch as He has given us life and has prepared the road ahead for us, the least we can do is glorify Him through the life that we live. I never truly knew love until I came to understand the incredible sacrifice that Jesus made to redeem my life. I similarly never truly experienced life until I received the promise of His indwelling Spirit. Traveling with the Holy Spirit directing my path has given me peace and joy that I'd never experienced prior to my conversion. The presence of the Holy Spirit has given purpose and fulfillment to my life.

God loves you and desires to accompany you in the same way. Whether you are a seeker or a mature believer, the cost is invariably the same. In order to complete your journey, it will cost you your life! You must eschew your former lifestyle and way of thinking in favor of the mind of Christ. It is the Holy Spirit who reveals the mind of Christ. If you give your life to Christ, He will fill you with His Spirit. As long as your heart and mind remain open to the leading of God's Spirit, nothing can stop you from reaching your divine destination.

●

Conclusion – The End of the Road

"I have fought a good fight, I have finished my course, I have kept the faith: Henceforth there is laid up for me a crown of righteousness, which the Lord, the righteous judge, shall give me at that day: and not to me only, but unto all them also that love his appearing." 2 Timothy 4:7-8, KJV

We began each section of the book with inspirational words from the Apostle Paul. Paul frequently compared life's journey to a long distance race. In section one, we read his admonishment to the Corinthians to run in such a way that they might win the race (1 Cor. 9:24). His sentiments reflect the importance of preparation and discipline as we strive toward important goals. In section two, we read how Paul instructed the Hebrews to set aside selfish ambitions and sinful ways that would impede their progress in life (Heb. 12:1). His advice reminds us that the proper attitude is essential to our success in life. In section three, we discussed Paul's transition from internal factors to external influences when he cautions the Philippians not to allow people or circumstances to discourage them along the way (Gal. 5:7). Paul's advice underscores the need for proper focus in life. In the final section, Paul encourages the Philippians to persevere to the finish (Phil. 3:13). In life we must learn to move past inevitable setbacks, knowing that God's grace will see us through to our destiny.

It is in the same spirit that Paul pens his final epistle written to his co-laborer and protégé, Timothy. Timothy was a faithful minister to Paul during much of his missionary work. After joining Paul during his second missionary journey, we find numerous references to Timothy in Paul's epistles. Paul affectionately referred to Timothy as his spiritual son, entrusting him with important assignments as they worked to establish the early church. It should come as no surprise that Paul's final letters are written to his beloved son in the gospel. Sensing that his death was imminent, Paul provided final words of encouragement to compel Timothy to finish his course.

Paul's final words to Timothy have a gravity that is only fully appreciated in the context of his life's work. As a primary agent for spreading the gospel to the Gentile world, Paul is firmly entrenched as a founding father of the early church. His incredible contribution to the cause of Christ is only matched by the fierce persecution that he faced and endured. As I have gained a better appreciation for Paul's journey in life, his parting words have a deeper meaning. Though weary physically and emotionally, Paul could confidently declare that he'd finished his course. Though it was a constant struggle until the end, Paul kept his faith in Christ and submitted to the leading of His Spirit. He made sure that Timothy was clear that this was the true measure of success.

Paul was not only certain that he'd completed his course, but he was persuaded that there was a just reward for his personal sacrifice. Paul described this reward as a crown of righteousness reserved just for him. Paul was alluding to his place in God's eternal kingdom. God's Word affirms that we must ultimately give account for our stewardship of the natural and spiritual resources that God entrusts to us. Did we spend our lives pursuing selfish ambitions or did we spend our lives doing the will of God? Paul knew he had done God's will. Therefore he is entitled not only to eternal life, but a position of prominence in God's kingdom. Paul reminds us that the promised reward is not exclusively reserved for him. Christ has reserved a special reward for everyone that submits to the leading of His Spirit and completes their God-ordained journey.

Paul's final letter serves not only as a charge to Timothy, but as a charge to each of us. Paul presents his own life as a testimony to the grace of God. It was through the power of God's indwelling Spirit that Paul led an exceptional life. His intimate relationship with God enriched his life and the lives of generations of men and women to this day. Whatever your plans are in life, I assure you that God's plans for you are greater. You must however resolve to submit to the leading of His Spirit so you can discover how great His plans truly are. May the grace of God overflow in your life as you embrace the charge to drive under the influence of His Spirit.

●

Epilogue

"But the gateway to life is small, and the road is narrow,
and only a few ever find it."
Matthew 7:14, NLT

We began our dialogue with a profound question offered by wise King Solomon. How does an individual find his or her way on the road of life? Solomon started us on the right path when he affirmed that it is God who determines our course. Using God's Word as my foundation, I have endeavored to establish a vitally important principle in life. God's Spirit is the only sure guide for life's journey. This is the primary function that the Holy Spirit serves in the lives of men and women, God's most precious creation. No other creation is offered the prospect of God's Spirit living on the inside. This intimate relationship could only be extended to the creature that was fashioned in His image and likeness.

Jesus Himself offers an essential perspective on life's journey as He speaks to us through His written word. Jesus tells us that the path that leads to eternal life is not easily uncovered. Firstly, He describes a small gate. A gate denotes access. Though numerous religions and philosophies purport to unlock the mysteries of life, access only comes through the acceptance of God's Word, which is personified in Jesus Christ. He similarly speaks of a narrow road. The road denotes the challenging course that one must follow to obtain eternal life. In order to follow a challenging course, a traveler must exercise wisdom and discipline. These attributes are also derived through application of God's Word. Though many people enter the great race of life, relatively few make their way to the finish. It is important to realize that a contestant's race can end before the course is completed. The Holy Spirit not only reveals the proper path but also empowers us to stay the course.

Jesus provides this perspective to encourage us and not to discourage us. If we better understand the nature of our journey and the sacrifice neces-sary to complete our assignment, we are more receptive to the agent who ensures our success. Jesus cares for us dearly. So much so that He offers us a piece of Himself to accompany us along the way. His Spirit is the essence of who He is — the invisible force that guards over His Word and affirms His promises.

My personal experience has taught me many things about the vital neces-sity of submitting to the leading of God's Spirit. I realized that it was impos-sible to determine the right path and proceed at the proper pace through my limited abilities. There was a period of my life when I tried various paths that all led to dead ends. It is most often the popular paths that lead to failure. The Holy Spirit has enabled me to uncover the less traveled path that leads to eternal life.

I understand that many people find it difficult to accept the premise of God's Spirit living in and working through them. For years I similarly strug-gled with this reality. The idea seemed too fantastic for my logical mind to grasp. This is commonly the case with many spiritual truths. God's indwell-ing Spirit is not a concept to be understood through reasoned explanation; rather it is a relationship that must be established through faith. It is only when we open our hearts that we experience the power and presence of God. Through experience we know that His Spirit is real and lives within us.

I'm proud to proclaim that God's Spirit lives inside of me. My boasting has nothing to do with me and everything to do with God's grace. When

I consider my life and the distance I've traveled, I am fully persuaded that God's Spirit has aided me along the way. The distance that I refer to is not measured by human standards. The distance I'm referring to is measured by spiritual growth with God's Word as my standard. My life has been transformed from the inside. As such, I have a new way of thinking that has led to a new direction. Each day my prayer is that God's Spirit will guide me as I make decisions that impact my life and the lives of others around me. I hope that I have encouraged you to either begin or continue to allow God's Spirit to lead you. If you ask for wisdom, God's Word will be revealed to you. If you seek God with your whole heart, you are certain to find Him. If you open your heart to God's Spirit, He will come in.

●

Acknowledgments

First giving praise and thanks to God and His indwelling Spirit that leads and guides me in all truth.

To my pastors and parents, Gary and Audrey Thomas. Through your example I've learned to follow the leading of God's Spirit.

To my gift from heaven and wonderful wife, Latania. Thank you for allowing God's Spirit to work through you enabling your perfect love for me.

To my sons, Javon and Micah, whom I love and cherish. Though I have the privilege of training you, you must allow God's Spirit to guide you.

To my siblings, Michael, Jarreon and Sayonnia. Let every step be ordered by the Lord.

To my uncle, Pastor Virgil Thomas. Thank you for being a living epistle exemplifying a life surrendered to the Holy Spirit.

To the great men and women of purpose who have helped me find my way on the road of life. Thank you.

To every individual that reads this book. I pray that it serves as a valuable resource and a reservoir of encouragement on your journey in this present life.

●

About the Author

Shundrawn A. Thomas, a native and resident of Chicago, Illinois, is a gifted strategist, executive, teacher, husband, and father. As a trusted advisor and motivational speaker, Shundrawn tirelessly uses his time and talent to empower and encourage individuals in the areas of faith, family, and finance. His previous release, *Ridiculous Faith* (Destiny Image $13.99), is considered by many to be a groundbreaking work on the concept of faith.

Professionally, Shundrawn serves as President and Chief Executive of Northern Trust Securities, Inc. a wholly owned subsidiary of Northern Trust Corporation. Previously, he served as Senior Vice President and Head of Corporate Strategy for the corporation. Northern Trust is a leading wealth management firm. Prior to joining Northern Trust, Shundrawn served as a Vice President for Goldman Sachs, a premiere investment banking firm. His principled business approach and dedication to excellence have made him an invaluable advisor to institutions and individuals.

Shundrawn is also an entrepreneur, previously serving as a founder and managing partner of Adelphos Holdings LLC, a business with Christian retail and publishing interests. He and his wife are currently the proprietors of another faith-based enterprise – Tree of Life Resources LLP, which develops multimedia content. Shundrawn is very involved in his local church, serving as a minister and board member. His church and community activism have afforded him numerous opportunities to speak locally and nationally on topics including Christian living, faith, marriage, education, leadership, values, strategy, entrepreneurship and personal finance.

Shundrawn serves on the Board of Trustees for Wheaton College. Additionally, he serves as a Board Director for the Florida A & M University Foundation, Communities in Schools Chicago and Urban Ministries, Inc. Shundrawn holds a Bachelor of Science in accounting from Florida A&M University. He holds a Masters of Business Administration from the University of Chicago's Booth School of Business. Shundrawn is happily married and enjoys spending time with his wife, Latania, and their sons, Javon and Micah.

•

For more information go to
www.ridiculousfaith.com
or contact us at
info@ridiculousfaith.com

CPSIA information can be obtained at www.ICGtesting.com
Printed in the USA
LVOW13s1610270514

387445LV00002B/470/P